Orchard

DEDICATION

JANE

> To Mum, Dad and Hare, with thanks
> for the lovely orchard of my childhood.

CHRIS

> To Janice, Philip and Charlie and the
> memory of the old orchard at my family
> home in Kent.

Jane McMorland Hunter
and Chris Kelly

Orchard

Growing and cooking fruit from your garden

PAVILION

Contents

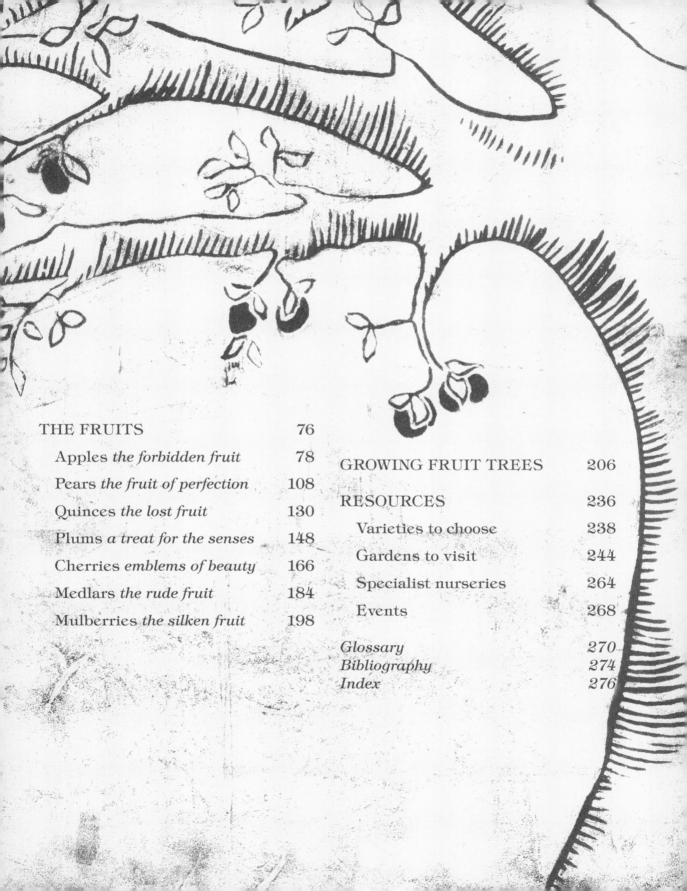

Introduction

What can your eye desire to see, your nose to smell, your mouth to take that is not to be had in an orchard.

William Lawson: *A New Orchard and Garden* 1618

Orchards are one of the oldest and most beautiful types of garden. Forget large commercial orchards and, instead, think of sitting in the gentle shade of a graceful tree and eating a perfect piece of fruit. You do not need a lot of space to achieve this; you don't even need much skill. Just a desire for really good fruit and a love of beautiful and civilised things.

In terms of availability, orchard fruits can be divided into two groups. Apples are the commonest fruit in northern Europe and available all year round; pears, plums and cherries are also easy to buy, but out of the hundreds of varieties that grow well in this region, shops rarely stock more than a few – choosing varieties for their looks and robustness rather than their taste and flavour. At the other end of the scale quinces are hard to find, and medlars and mulberries almost impossible. The way to get the best of all these fruits is to grow your own. Nothing beats the taste of an exactly ripe, juicy pear eaten straight from the tree or a fluffy baked apple.

Whether you have a tiny balcony or a huge field, you can easily grow apples, pears, plums, quinces, cherries, medlars or even a mulberry tree. Most are remarkably unfussy and their huge range means that there is a variety for most situations. The majority will have been grafted onto a rootstock that will determine the final size of the plant. This means that, within reason, you can have the type of fruit you want on a size of tree you can accommodate in your

6 INTRODUCTION

garden. All fruit trees have beautiful blossom in the spring, but you need to consider carefully what sort of fruit you want. Apples divide into cookers, dessert, cider and crab, but there is a great range within each group. Most early cropping eaters like Beauty of Bath are best eaten straight from the tree, whereas later varieties, such as Ashmead's Kernel will keep for several months. Dual apples like James Grieve are suitable for eating or cooking and, on a more specialised note, Reine de Reinettes (King of the Pippins) has been developed to make the perfect *tarte tatin*! Court Pendu Plat or Wise Apple (so called because its late flowering avoided any frosts) is an ancient variety, mentioned in many 16th-century gardening manuals, and probably introduced by the Romans. Whereas Greensleeves is a recent cross between Golden Delicious and James Grieve, producing disease-resistant dual apples. Cider apple trees tend to be larger, and you really need to grow several if you want to make a decent amount of cider. However, a single small crab apple will fertilise easily, give you exquisite blossom and fruit for jelly in the autumn. There is a similarly mind-boggling range of varieties for pears, plums and cherries, and even quinces, medlars and mulberries run to double figures. The choice goes on and on, and is almost endless when one considers the hundreds of varieties that were historically grown but have fallen out of favour and only survive in specialist orchards, such as Brogdale in Kent or Potager du Roy at Versailles. Too much information can be as confusing as too little and we have chosen a selection of trees which should provide something for everyone.

If you have limited space you can easily grow fruit trees in containers and train them against a wall or fence. This way they won't take up more than a few inches of your garden, but will provide a beautiful backdrop throughout the year. If you have room for several trees, or even an orchard, you can choose trees so that their flowering and fruiting seasons are staggered. This means you will enjoy a longer season of blossom, and will avoid a glut when everything ripens at once. Each fruit has its own fascinating history and, over the years, many have taken on important symbolic and mythological roles around the world.

For many people, the history of apples begins with the forbidden fruit in the Garden of Eden. There is considerable doubt that the Tree of Knowledge was an apple and their history actually goes back much further to the forests of the Tien Shan region of central Asia. Here, apples and many other fruits, have grown wild on the hillsides for more than 7,000 years. Since apple trees do not grow true from seed, every tree that grows there is different to its parent. The resulting forests of wild fruit trees range from some that are little more than tiny shrubs to others that tower 15m (50ft) in the sky, each bearing different fruit. It is this diversity that has enabled apples to settle so well right across the temperate regions of the world. Travellers and merchants passing along the ancient Silk Route spread apples to the East and West, both

Right: This Roman 3rd-century mosaic covers the floor of the triclinium (dining room) in the Africa House at Thysdrus (now El Djem) in Tunisia.

intentionally as they found good fruits, and unintentionally as their horses and camels ate the fruit and deposited the seeds further along the track.

From their exotic origins apples have taken on important symbolic roles. They can be found in paintings as diverse as Lucas Cranach's *Adam and Eve* and Magritte's *The Son of Man*. Poets such as Robert Frost have celebrated apples, and they appear in more nursery rhymes and traditional songs than any other fruit. They were the source of Isaac Newton's discovery of gravity, Prince Ahmed's cure for all ills in the *Tales from the Arabian Nights*, and the fruit that nearly killed Snow White in Grimms' *Fairy Tales*. On a commercial level, two major icons of the 20th-century, the Beatles and Apple Computers, linked their worldwide businesses to this fruit.

Apples can be made into jams and chutneys and dried for storage, and their culinary uses extend well beyond traditional pies and crumbles. Like many fruits, apples complement savoury foods and can be used in delicious and diverse recipes. Juices include everything from the innocent to the highly alcoholic. Apples are nutritious, and their use against scurvy is well known. What is less well known is their use for improving your complexion and even reducing wrinkles!

The desirability of pears is enhanced by their perishability. More shapely than apples, and harder to come by, pears have always been a highly prized fruit. They also originated in central Asia and, like so many other things, were spread around Europe by the Romans. By the 11th-century they were popular throughout France, and the Normans embarked on pear growing on a grand scale when they invaded Britain in 1066. The best way to get a perfect pear is to pick it straight from the tree and although improved transportation meant that it was possible to get pears to the central markets of the growing towns and cities, they rarely arrived in an ideal state. Apart from dessert pears, you can also grow cooking and perry pears. It would be a crime to cook with a perfect dessert pear, as Edward Bunyard, the pomologist, wrote in his book *The Anatomy of Dessert*: '*I begin with a confession. After thirty years of tasting pears I am still unfurnished with a vocabulary to describe the flavour.*' Cooking pears are very versatile, and mix well with such diverse ingredients as almonds and Stilton, making them suitable for both sweet and savoury dishes. You can also make perry or pear liqueurs.

The plums cultivated in Europe originated in western Asia around the Caucasus, but their ancestors, sloes and bullaces, have thrived everywhere for thousands of years. Bullace stones have been found on prehistoric sites, and sloes are common in ancient hedges. The fruits of both tend to be very sharp, but make wonderful jams, jellies and, of course,

Above: Quinces, neatly packed for storage or transport. Although the fruits appear rock hard, they bruise very easily.

liqueurs. Cultivated plums further divide into damsons and greengages, or gages, as they are often known. Cultivated damsons came from the area around Damascus, and were brought back to Britain by the Crusaders in the 12th-century. Greengages are simply particularly fine green plums. They grew in the region in Roman times but were lost during the Dark Ages. In 1724, they were 'discovered' by Sir Thomas Gage when his brother gave him some from France. The individual name arose because they were referred to as green Gage's plums, whereas in France they were simply classified as a variety of plum. Plums became especially popular during Henry VIII's reign and 5,000 were found on his warship *The Mary Rose.* Similar varieties can be seen growing today at Canons Ashby House in Northamptonshire. Throughout the 19th-century, plum orchards covered much of the west Midlands and north-west of England, partly as a fruit crop and partly for dyes for the woollen industry. Like so many others, most of these orchards have now sadly vanished. In the kitchen, plums and damsons make wonderful jams, but can also be made into ice cream and served with meat and game.

Quinces, or *Cydonia,* originally came to Europe from central Asia where they grow wild in the foothills of the Caucasus Mountains in Turkestan and Iran. They have been used in Persian cooking for more than 2,500 years, but probably reached Britain in the 13th-century where they appear in recipes for pies sweetened with honey. References date to even further back in history: they were reputed to be the fruit that Paris gave Aphrodite, and it was said that quince trees grew up wherever she walked. Much later, in 1871, Edward Lear's Owl and Pussycat dined on quinces at their wedding feast.

Our apples were stored in old stockings, which hung eerily from the beams in the shed, creating the image of a crowd of dumpy people in the rafters above.

JANE

Quinces are deliciously sweet and scented when cooked. They contain a high level of pectin and can, therefore, easily be made into jams and jellies. Originally, marmalade was made from quinces; it comes from the Portuguese word for the fruit: marmelo. A little goes a long way, and the addition of a few slices will transform sweet and savoury dishes. Quinces combine particularly well with apples and pears, but will also enhance almonds, oranges, and even mulberries, if you can get them. They can be made into cakes, pies, shortbread and fools. They are used in many Mediterranean and central Asian savoury dishes, with chicken, beef and all types of game. They can be stuffed with meat or cheese, and used to flavour savoury tarts. There is so much more to them than just the jelly and cheese commonly found in delicatessens. Before you cook them, quinces can be used to scent a room. Once ripened, they are an attractive yellow to gold colour and will keep in a bowl for months, giving off a delightful fragrance.

Cherry trees are deservedly renowned for their beautiful spring blossom, but if you grow sweet or sour cherries, you will have the benefit of the blossom as well as the added bonus of fruit. Sour or Morello cherries are unusual amongst fruit trees in that they will happily grow in the shade or against a north-facing wall, making them ideal for many awkward sites.

In northern Europe, wild cherries date back to prehistoric times, and sour cherries have been cultivated here continuously since the Romans arrived. They originally brought the fruit from central Asia, and the Latin name is thought to come from the Italian port of Cersasus where the fruit was landed in the first-century BC. Alternatively, it may have originated from karsu, an Accadian word used by the Assyrians and Babylonians who first cultivated the fruit. Sweet or eating cherries were popular in Europe and reached Britain via Flanders in Tudor times. Dukes are a later introduction still and are a cross between sweet and sour cherries.

From the Middle Ages right up to the end of the 19th-century, cherry fairs were one of the major rural festivals throughout Britain. Fruit was picked and sold, and dancing, drinking and merry making in general took place in the orchards. Cherry trees have long been a potent symbol for lovers, from the ancient Willow Pattern china to Shakespeare's *A Midsummer Night's Dream* and D. H. Lawrence's *Sons and Lovers*. Chekhov's *The Cherry Orchard* is probably the fruit's best literary claim to fame with the impoverished Russian aristocratic family refusing to give up their ancient family orchard.

In the kitchen, cherries are as adaptable as any of the orchard fruits, making scrumptious puddings, and also complement savoury dishes of all types of game. Cherries feature in drinks such as kirsch, cherry brandy and true maraschino liqueur.

Medlars are the lost fruits of the orchard. Popular in the Middle Ages, they are now regarded as quirky looking, unpalatable and unusable, other than as jelly. This is unfair. The fruit does have an acquired taste, but it can be used in a number of ways beyond jelly, and the trees themselves are almost unbelievably charming. They are small, have exquisite blossom, extraordinary fruits, stunning autumn colour and, in winter, their dark, twisty branches will grace any view. They are also extremely long lived. A Nottingham variety, planted in the 17th-century by James I, was still alive at the end of the 20th-century.

They have probably been cultivated for more than 3,000 years, but there is a certain amount of confusion as the word medlar was used to describe the cornelian cherry, stone fruits in general and the hawthorn, to which the medlar is closely related. It was traditionally thought that medlars originated along the west coast of the Caspian Sea, but leaf impressions have been found in interglacial deposits in eastern Germany, so their origins may in fact be much older and more European.

Mespilus, the Latin name for medlar, comes from two Greek words, *mesos* meaning half and *pilos* meaning ball, but due to the suggestive shape of the fruit these trees have many, much ruder, common names. In France they are known as *cul de chien* (dog's bottom), and in medieval Britain they were called 'open-arse' or 'openers'. When writing *Romeo and Juliet* Shakespeare refined this to '*open et cetera*'.

The trees became very popular in the Middle Ages, with Charlemagne making their inclusion mandatory on royal estates, and they are still found in many ancient monastery gardens. The fruit was traditionally eaten with port or wine after a meal, but was also highly regarded medicinally. The Chinese believe that tea made from the seeds will improve your eyesight, while in Britain they were credited with many properties including strengthening the memory, aiding digestion, preventing miscarriages and, as Culpeper so neatly put it: '*The fruit eaten by women with child will stayeth their longing after unusual meats... and make them joyful mothers.*'

The fruit never ripens fully in northern Europe and needs to be bletted before it can be eaten. This simply means stored until the fruit has softened and usually takes a couple of weeks. Opinion is then divided as to the palatability of the flesh, with D. H. Lawrence describing the ripe fruits as '*wineskins of brown morbidity*'. They are often said to resemble rotten apples, but the flavour is really a more desirable mixture of apples, dates and cinnamon, and is delicious scooped out and served with cream and sugar.

Above: In this orchard the trees have been kept fairly low so that the fruit can be easily picked. The wide paths in between allow easy access to the trees, a good circulation of air and, later in the year, a carpet of meadow flowers to grow up.

Mulberries are not true orchard fruits, but the beauty of the trees and the pleasure the fruit brings, earn them a place in this book. They are best grown in the centre of a lawn where you will get the full benefit of the shape of the tree, but they are accommodating plants and can be espaliered against a sunny wall in colder areas, or grown in pots if space is tight. Growing old in looks before their time, they quickly develop a gnarled and twisted framework giving you a tree that looks as if it has graced your garden for five hundred years when it is only twenty years old.

Like so many other fruits in this book, it originated in central Asia, spread across Europe and were brought to Britain by the Romans. Although, it was in the early 17th-century that mulberries really spread here when King James I decided to make his a silk-growing nation. Thousands of black mulberries were planted the length and breadth of the kingdom, but sadly the silk production was only partly successful. King James, or rather his advisers, had failed to realise that there are two types of mulberry, black and white; while the black produces wonderful, juicy fruit, it is the white that is preferred by silkworms. The Italians were more successful (as they planted the right type of mulberries) in the area around Lucca.

The fruits are so juicy that they do not travel well and are almost impossible to buy. Delicious eaten straight from the tree, they also make wonderful jam, interesting wine and will enhance any fruit pudding. The Romans even used them in a sauce on poached fish.

Increasingly, we are becoming aware of the fact that local produce has a better flavour, and this is especially true for orchard fruits. One can travel around Britain and parts of Europe and, county by county and country by country, find individual varieties of fruit that are specific to each area. If you visit local orchards and nurseries, you will discover a wealth of different trees, many of which may not exist anywhere else. Plant a fruit tree and in return you will have exquisite blossom in the spring, fabulous fruit in the autumn and a beautiful tree to sit under on hot, sunny afternoons.

Right: Ballerina trees in tubs allow you to have apple trees on even the tiniest balcony.

A Brief History of Orchards

The earliest orchards were really walled and irrigated fruit gardens in ancient Persia and Egypt, set out on a formal grid pattern of canals. Typically, they would have grown figs, dates, pomegranates and vines. Fragmentary poems, written in Egypt before 1080 BC, on a document known as the Turin Papyrus, describe what seems to be one such garden of delights. The poet praises the sensuous qualities of the fruit, appreciating the transience and seasonality of flowering, ripening and re-growth, while comparing the pomegranate fruit to his lover's breasts and its seeds to her teeth.

It is laden with the ripeness of notched figs,
Redder than cornelian,
Like turquoise in its leaves,
Like glass its bark.

In the 6th-century, King Darius I of Persia encouraged growing fruit trees in enclosures known as *pairidaeza*, the source of the Greek world paradeisos. As apple expert Joan Morgan has written, of a *'vision of paradise – an enclosure filled with fruit trees watered by pools and canals... an image of beauty combined with utility that has never left orchards and fruit trees.'* This proved to be enormously influential, probably because

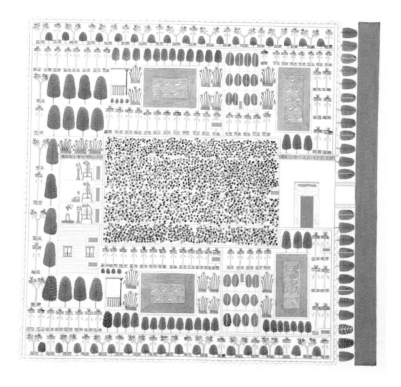

it combined utility with an appeal to the strongest human emotions. The description of Eden, full of every type of tree and plant, must have been influenced by similar gardens. Certainly, the human desire to create an earthly paradise was inspired by the story of The Garden of Eden throughout Christian Europe, while many Islamic gardens can trace their origins to these early paradises.

ORCHARDS OD ANCIENT GREECE

Mediterranean myths evolved from the surrounding natural world. Ripening fruits' curving, soft, sensuous surfaces were metaphors for the feelings of lust, sensuality, delight, or guilt or shame that pervade every culture. By the first millennium BC sacred groves or collections of fruit trees had become important in mythology, with apples, pears and quinces predominating. Arguably, the greatest storyteller of all time, Homer, reflects on the significance of orchards in human experience. Odysseus, after years of wandering around the Mediterranean, finally returns to his native Ithaca, to find it in unfriendly hands.

Earlier on his voyage, he saw the magnificent, almost jewel-like orchard belonging to Alcinous, King of the Phaeacians, which brought back bitter memories of his distant homeland. His homecoming confronts him with a more modest, but, even more emotionally charged place. While searching for his family, he comes disguised and unrecognised to a small orchard where his aged father, Laertes, is tending his fruit trees. He reveals his identity but is not believed. He offers proof: first he shows a scar upon his forehead, and then he describes the exact number of the trees in the orchard, given to him by his father when he was a child.

> *Yet by another sign thy offspring know*
> *The several trees you gave me long ago*
> *While yet a child, these fields I loved to trace*
> *And trod thy footsteps with unequal pace*
> *To every plant in order as we came*
> *Well-pleased you told its nature and its name*
> *Whate'er my childish fancy asked, bestow'd:*
> *Twelve pear-trees, bowing with their pendant load,*
> *And ten, that red with blushing apples glowed!*

ORCHARDS OF ANCIENT ROME

Orchards and fruit trees spread slowly, from Asia and the Middle East through the Mediterranean, from Greece to Rome and to the fringes of western Europe. The Romans grew so much fruit it was said that Italy was one vast orchard. They also wrote about growing it. Amongst the most famous authors are Columella and Virgil – who writes of the cultivation and grafting of fruit trees in his *Georgics*. Pliny offered extensive cultural advice and, in his famous description of his villa, wrote about '*little apple trees*' set amidst topiarised plants. These famous classical passages became well known amongst educated European elites of the Renaissance onwards. They were probably an influence not only in the general development of gardens and country estates, but also on the specific inclusion of fruit trees within the domestic and privy gardens of great houses and palaces.

EARLY ORCHARDS IN BRITAIN

There is good archeological evidence (stones and pips) that fruit had been eaten in Britain long before the Romans arrived, but little proof of its cultivation. The Romans, spreading their culture wherever feasible, almost certainly grew fruit trees in Britain. Tacitus, for example, tells us how the climate was not suitable for olives, but doesn't say anything about fruit trees, implying that he was dealing only with exceptions. At the least they are likely to have grown apples, pears, plums and perhaps quinces.

Fruit growing has spread across the globe by an uneven process, checked or driven forward in turns by trade, wars, climate, disease or changes in taste and demand. Once the great voyages of discovery began at the end of the 15th-century, colonisation led to demand for fruit trees and orchards wherever conditions would support them. Long before then, however, the Roman Empire finally gave way.

MONASTERY ORCHARDS

Once Rome fell, trade and agriculture declined and instability grew. To thrive, orchards need predictable, long-term demand for fruit, and protection from pillage and destruction, so they suffered heavily throughout western Europe. In Britain, the vital continuity and care in uncertain times were offered by monasteries, which were established from the time of Saint Augustine in the late 6th-century. Monastic orchards were places of contemplation; they were symbolic of the pre-fall Eden and many aspects of the Christian life. An idealised plan for an orchard at the Monastery of St Gall in Switzerland

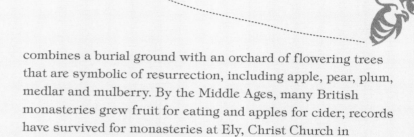

combines a burial ground with an orchard of flowering trees that are symbolic of resurrection, including apple, pear, plum, medlar and mulberry. By the Middle Ages, many British monasteries grew fruit for eating and apples for cider; records have survived for monasteries at Ely, Christ Church in Canterbury (c.1165) and Battle in Somerset (1275).

MEDIEVAL ORCHARDS OUTSIDE THE MONASTERIES

Fruit was also grown outside monasteries. There were substantial royal orchards at Windsor. When Robert the Bruce besieged Carlisle in 1315, he failed to take the city, but spitefully destroyed the fruit trees cultivated outside its walls. The later medieval period was a bad time for fruit growing. First droughts, and then the Black Death of 1347, hit supply and restricted demand, while agricultural wages rose considerably in the competition to employ surviving workers.

Medieval illustrations from 15th-century Continental Europe show fruit-laden trees as essential components of a noble orchard garden, along with turf benches, flowers and paths. Such orchards were an appropriate setting for the flowering of courtly love and its associated and often carnal flirtations, described at length in texts such as the *Romance of the Rose* (Chaucer's translation uses familiar English names for the fruits and trees involved). Similar courtly orchards or pleasure gardens probably existed in England, too.

TUDOR ORCHARDS

After 1485, Tudor rule re-established political stability, and gradually the creation of gardens and orchards became easier, while Renaissance influences slowly filtered in through France. From the 1520s until the mid-18th-century, fruit growing prospered and we can start to distinguish separate trends in orchards. Firstly, commercial fruit growing developed rapidly until the mid-18th-century. Secondly, magnificent

orchards were planted in the gardens and palaces of the rich. Thirdly, ordinary domestic pleasure orchards flourished, influenced by the great aristocratic gardens, but without their political symbolism and show.

Growth in orchards and cider making corresponded with the publication of many books on the subject. By 1565, William Harrison praised the high point reached by British orchards, and the variety and the quality of British fruit. In 1618, William Lawson wrote delightfully of the pleasures of orchards, using language that implied they had been established amongst the middle classes for some generations – as well as benefiting from the lead in fruit breeding and fashionable gardening amongst the rich and aristocratic. After the Restoration, John Rea, adopting a more scientific tone, declared that gardeners should be forced to plant orchards, as well as advising on methods of increasing yields.

Commercial orchards flourished from the reign of Henry VIII onwards, spurred on by imports of better quality fruit trees, principally from France. They got a major stimulus in 1533 when Richard Harris, Henry VIII's fruiterer, set up commercial orchards at Teynham in Kent, using trees obtained from Normandy that he propagated in other suitable areas. Farmers' orchards were mainly planted with cooking and coarser eating fruit, especially apples, pears and plums. Planting was on a grand scale, with a substantial distance (perhaps as much as 20m/60ft) between tall standard trees. On more valuable land in Kent (perhaps close to large cities, with access to London markets via river transport), the quality of tree and fruit was correspondingly better. Greater market opportunities and land values also justified more intensive farming, and trees were under-planted with other market-garden crops.

THE GREAT TUDOR AND STUART PLEASURE ORCHARDS
By the 1520s, the use of fruit trees within pleasure gardens
had expanded well beyond the level of the late medieval period.
Most written records and illustrations relate to royal palaces
and the gardens of great aristocrats. They show that in the
first half of the 16th-century such gardens often included
an essentially ornamental orchard, constructed as part of a
display of magnificence intended to demonstrate the might,
riches and political rightness of the ruling family and their
key courtiers.

At Thornbury Castle in Gloucestershire, built and planted
by the third Duke of Buckingham before his execution in 1521,
there was *'a large and goodly orchard full of young graffes well
laden with frute, many roses and other pleasures; and in the same
orchard are many goodly alies to walk ynn openly; and rounde
about the same orchard is conveyed on a good heighte other alies
with roosting places covered thoroughly with whitethorn and
basil.'* The trees were part of a mixed planting, along with
roses and hedging, formally laid out within an enclosed space,
and you could walk through them on set paths or see them from
above, from the covered walkways surrounding the garden.
It was a pleasure orchard as much as a working one, but the
fruit no doubt got eaten! Shakespeare probably had something
similar in mind when he wrote of Capulet's orchard in *Romeo
and Juliet*.

At Hampton Court in 1531, the Privy Orchard contained
seven sun dials, and was ornamented by a number of painted
wooden Kinges Bestes or heraldic animals, such as dragons,
greyhounds, lions, horses and antelopes. Other important
pleasure orchards of the period were at Hatfield House,
Theobalds in Hertfordshire, and the earlier Wilton House
in Wiltshire. In the 120 odd years from Thornbury's
establishment until the Civil War began, fruit trees
continued to be an essential component of great gardens.

However, their exact function was influenced by Italian ideas, often transmitted through France. Decorative and useful roles were often combined in the techniques of espaliering and training, so that trees could line garden walls, or form precise avenues of formally shaped bushes.

By 1611, at Hatfield, the head gardener was the famous plantsman John Tradescant, who received 500 fruit trees from his equivalent at the French court. They were sent by Anne of Austria, wife of Louis XIII of France, together with three under gardeners to see that they were planted properly! In 1612, Hatfield acquired 453 cherry trees. Such precise records are unusual. Successful fruit nurseries had been established in Britain in the second half of the 16th-century, but it is not certain that they could have fulfilled an order of this size as easily as the French Royal Gardens.

In 1639, when Charles I bought Wimbledon Manor for his queen, Henrietta Maria, work had just begun to separate the orchard proper, of some 10 acres, from the palace's delectable pleasure orchard, which was set with cherries and fountains, and in which fruit trees were but one element of the whole.

WILLIAM LAWSON AND DOMESTIC STUART ORCHARDS

In ordinary Tudor homes displays of wealth and power were less important: an orchard simply became a pleasant part of the garden of many minor gentry and yeomen, valued as much for its atmosphere of peace and calm as for the fruit it produced.

A precise description of this sort of pleasure orchard is given in William Lawson's A New Orchard and Garden, published in 1618. Lawson was clearly writing about an established type of orchard garden that could have developed over 50 or 60 years, when he depicts one such compartmentalised orchard with ornamental knots, topiary, a fountain, bee hives and, at the corners, mounts or artificial hills to look down from.

Previous page: This walled garden looks especially pretty in spring with the apple blossom. Within the walls, the garden – and particularly the fruit trees – will be protected from the worst of any cold weather.

Right: A plan showing the ornamental and productive gardens on the north side of a house in William Lawson's A New Orchard and Garden, written in 1618.

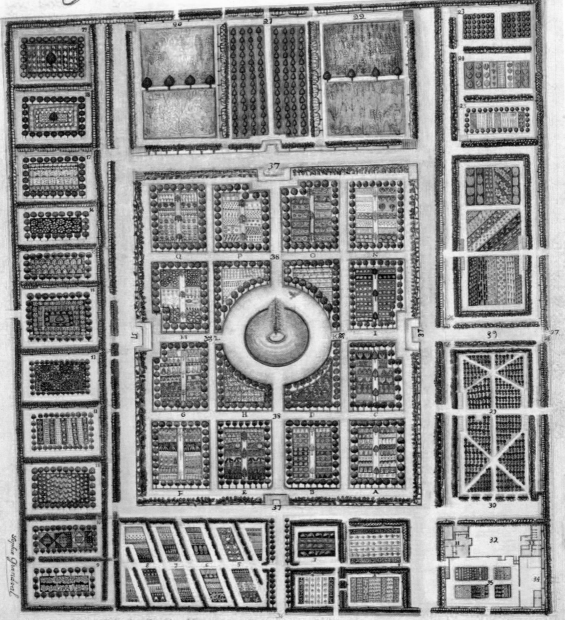

Le Jardin Potager du Roi à Versailles

His writing is much quoted, and with every reason, by garden historians for its combination of the pleasures of the senses, the intellect and the orchard's place in history. He writes of planting the orchard with *'an infinite variety of sweet smelling flowers... decking with sundry colours the green mantle of the earth... The rose red, damask velvet and double double province rose... The fair and sweet senting woodbine... the violet for scenting sweetly...'* and goes on to describe the side borders as *'hanging and drooping with Feberries* [gooseberries]*, raspberries, barberries, currans and the roots of your trees powdered with strawberries, red, white and green. What pleasure is this?'* Lawson then describes a sentiment that must be very common to all orchard owners, even if seldom recorded, letting them *'retreat from the troublesome affaires of their estate... to renue and refresh their sences and to call home their over-wearied spirits.'*

ORCHARDS AFTER THE CIVIL WAR

By the Restoration in 1660, a more scientific and rational approach to fruit growing in particular and things in general, had begun. It was now harder to see the paradise of which Lawson wrote, when he described it as *'but a Garden and Orchard of trees and herbs, full of pleasures... and nothing there but delights.'* The gains of increased productivity and quality of fruit were offset by the, arguably, greater loss: what had formerly been a *'more sublime conception of the Universe'*. The great age of the orchard as pleasure garden was coming to an end.

Technical improvements in fruit growing continued to spread throughout the 17th-century, often originating in France (where they were first developed in medieval monasteries), and reaching England through translations of French books. Growing fruit against walls, training the trees into attractive, highly productive shapes and dwarfing them were all prominent elements of this trend. Two of the surviving

Left: This ink and watercolour plan shows the exact layout of *Le Jardin Potager du Roi* (Louis XIV's vegetable garden) at Versailles.

French late 17th-century fruit gardens, one in the Potager Royal at Versailles and another in the Jardins de Luxembourg in central Paris, show these techniques at their finest and really deserve a visit. In Britain, two post-Restoration gardens which used trained fruit trees in an essentially baroque manner, have been replanted recently, using old varieties of fruit trees, by the National Trust. Westbury Court in Gloucestershire has a predominantly Dutch-influenced garden with a long canal, while Erddig in Wales demonstrates how the grand, French baroque manner was adapted in the English provinces. It is exceptionally lucky that these gardens have not been altogether swept away by changes in fashion.

FRUIT GROWING OUTSIDE EUROPE FOR THE 1660s
ONWARDS
Fruit growing spread steadily as the known world expanded. Newly discovered lands led to new empires, and the process of colonisation drove agricultural development in all forms. This certainly included fruit trees. In North America, early attempts to set up orchards had been made from 1625 or so onwards, but met with rather mixed results, given the prevailing harsh conditions and sometimes unstable local relations. By the 18th-century, however, orchards were doing well in what would become the USA after the War of Independence. The costs and difficulties of transporting trees across the Atlantic led to a greater dependency on growing fruit from seeds, and this seems to have been responsible or the evolution of many new, and often highly successful, varieties – especially of apples – suited to the harsh winter climates. The Prince Fruit Nursery, the first of its type, had been established by 1737 in Long Island and by the 1770s was supplying trees to Thomas Jefferson's magnificent new gardens at Monticello. The USA in general saw remarkable growth in fruit production in the first half of the 19th-

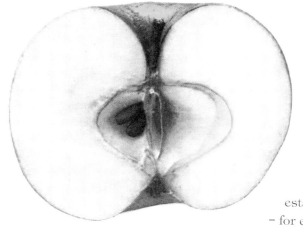

Above: A Mann apple from Beach's *Apples of New York*.

century, much of which is recorded in some fine contemporary illustrated books, such as Beach's *Apples of New York*.

During the 19th-century orchards were established in Australia, where climate permitted – for example, in Tasmania – and New Zealand. All of these countries have become major, cost-effective exporters of high-quality fruit to European markets: a factor in the decline of British commercial orchards. South America and China are now successful exporters, too: imported Chinese apple juice is used for a significant proportion of UK cider manufacture.

COUNTRY HOUSE ORCHARDS AND FRUIT GARDENS IN BRITAIN DURING THE 18TH-CENTURY

On large estates and even amongst the prosperous middle classes, the trend for training and growing fruit trees against (sometimes heated) walls spread, while the fruit garden became architecturally isolated from the house, as the 18th-century progressed. Separate walled fruit gardens and orchards of the highest quality, but well-removed from the mansion they served, were the norm by the mid-18th-century. They were driven away from the main house by the preference for an uncluttered landscape – as well as removing the smell of manure, used to heat the forcing frames for exotics such as melons and pineapples. The cult of fruit gardens for the rich finally peaked in the late 19th- and early 20th-century, fuelled by money, technical excellence and demand for the highest-quality fruit for a separate dessert course. This form of connoisseurship declined quite rapidly, along with the gardening skills to meet it, after the First

World War. Some of these walled fruit gardens, have been
preserved and restored (see Gardens to Visit) and are well
worth a visit.

FRUIT TREES IN GARDENS SINCE THE MID-18TH-CENTURY

Once fashion, in the form of the landscape movement, had
swept aside many earlier gardens in the mid-18th-century, there
seems to have been a period of at least a hundred years when it
was not customary to plant fruit trees as part of a mixed
garden (as opposed to specialised fruit gardens and orchards).
However, the Romantic Movement and the inability of the
19th-century to define its own style, fostered many eclectic
architectural revivals that copied features from, and attempted
to emulate the spirit of, much earlier buildings and styles. The
historicist movement aspired to produce gardens that evoked
aspects of the Medieval, Tudor and Stuart periods, such as
Haddon Hall. At Hatfield, the then Lord Salisbury, returning
to an effectively abandoned property, recreated the Jacobean
terraces, albeit somewhat out of scale, in preparation for a visit
from Queen Victoria in 1846. Much more recently, the (now)
Dowager Lady Salisbury, has recalled and honoured the
influence of John Tradescant by planting two fine apple
walks, a formal orchard, and numerous pleached apples and
fan-trained pears grown against old walls. Although nothing
has been copied, a great deal of the spirit has been revived.

Likewise at Penshurst in Kent, the de Lisle family maintains
frequent plantings of fruit trees (some of which appear to be
of considerable age) in a famous mixed garden of great charm,
restored in the 1860s (using Kip's engraving of c.1700 as a
guide), and again reworked in the 1970s onwards. The gardens
and orchards were praised by both Ben Jonson in 1616 and
John Evelyn who, recording a visit in his diary for 9 July
1652, stated it was 'famous once for its gardens and excellent
fruit'. Jonson had earlier written:

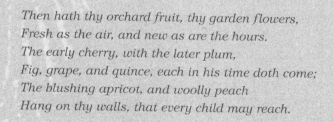

Then hath thy orchard fruit, thy garden flowers,
Fresh as the air, and new as are the hours.
The early cherry, with the later plum,
Fig, grape, and quince, each in his time doth come;
The blushing apricot, and woolly peach
Hang on thy walls, that every child may reach.

Fruit trees also underwent a renaissance as part of the
Arts and Crafts movement, towards the end of the 19th-century,
with its emphasis on rediscovering medieval purity through
supposed simplicity. In this case, tapestry and manuscript
illustrations probably provided an imaginative springboard.
This movement was a formative influence on some fine efforts
in orchard revival, such as the project at Tyninghame, East
Lothian. Records show that Lord Binning planted a fruit tunnel,
144yd (132m), long entirely with Keswick Codlin apples,
which are as attractive for their blossom as for their fruit.

This century many garden designers have incorporated fruit
trees into their plantings, often to mark the centre or corners
of formal layouts in garden rooms; but generally they have been
but one ingredient in a far more mixed whole, albeit giving
shade, texture, shape and form – as well as blossom and fruit.

COMMERCIAL FRUIT GROWING IN BRITAIN IN THE 18TH-CENTURY

Commercial fruit growing in Britain declined in the mid-18th-
century because of the greater profitability of corn and stock
farming, and recurring outbreaks of disease, such as canker
in fruit trees. But increased local demand sometimes led to a
boom that bucked the overall trend. As new cities developed,
access to markets became easier, first through canal networks
(and subsequently the 19th-century railways), and new areas
of high-quality cultivation emerged, such as Pershore in
Worcestershire, to meet increased demand.

COMMERCAIL FRUIT GROWING IN BRITAIN IN THE 19TH & 20TH CENTURIES

The Napoleonic Wars brought about a more general improvement. Import tariffs protected domestic fruit and there was a great campaign of breeding new varieties among country gentlemen anxious to improve their estates. An associated phenomenon, both then and in the later 19th-century, was the production of very splendid, and splendidly expensive, pomonas (fruit books illustrated with coloured plates) which now command many thousands of pounds at auction. Some of the magnificent plates are reproduced throughout this book.

The removal of import tariffs in 1837 was enough to trigger another decline, only reversed by the rising prosperity of the later 19th-century, and the excellent efforts of both amateur enthusiast and scientists to improve fruit breeding and growing, as well as cider production. Again, a period of great enthusiasm spread throughout the whole country, in a patriotic defiance of American imports that had threatened to swamp the market. The great nurseryman, Thomas Rivers, and the Laxton family were responsible for developing new varieties of apples, pears and plums – some of the best varieties are still grown today. Their role was eventually taken up by state-sponsored fruit research stations in the past century. Unfortunately, by the time the First World War ended, a more serious decline in fruit growing set in, and cheap imports claimed an increasing share of the market. Orchards were turned over to other uses or developed for building, as the land value rose and fruit growing offered less tempting returns.

The later 20th-century saw an even greater reduction in commercial fruit growing in the Britain, largely a consequence of globalisation. Production costs are lower in nations such as China and potential economies of scale are greater. British growers cannot compete on price while overseas transport costs remain relatively low. Only a fraction of the areas once

Previous page: This shows part
of Thomas Jefferson's extensive fruit
gardens at his Monticello estate
in Charlottesville, Virginia. When
they were originally laid out in the
late 18th-century the fruit and
vegetable gardens covered an
extensive area, taking inspiration
from the French and British gardens
Jefferson had visited.

Left: The frost on this beautiful,
ornamental flowering quince
(*Chaenomeles*) looks wonderful.
However, fruit trees must be
protected during the colder months
so that the crop is not lost.

planted as orchards remain. Between 1877 and 1979, the
acreage covered by cider apple orchards in Herefordshire
and Worcestershire alone was reduced by 80 per cent. Where
commercial orchards remain, most trees are much smaller
than the old standards, more closely planted, and trained as
bushes for earlier yields and easier picking. The result is an
efficiently run, but much less pretty orchard. EU regulations
and agricultural policy hasn't helped either; subsidies have
been paid for ploughing up orchards to put land to other
agricultural uses. The victims of this policy are the valuable
and scarce varieties of fruit trees, and the habitat they create.

RECENT ORCHARD RESTORATIONS
Since the Second World War, several garden restoration
projects in the UK and abroad have used old varieties of fruit
trees in an attempt to create the feel and layout of 17th- and
early 18th-century orchards (for example, the National Trust
at Westbury in Gloucestershire, and Erddig in Wales), coming
as close to historical accuracy as can reasonably be expected.
Old planting lists have been helpful. The 1718 and 1724 lists
for Erddig, apparently, contain plums with the wonderful
names of Gush Madam and Blue Pedrigon! (See Patrick
Taylor's book Period Gardens, published by Pavilion in 1991.)

   In the USA, Jefferson's orchard at Monticello was carefully
surveyed in post-Second World War restoration work, one
of the rare times when it has been possible to recreate the
intentions of the original designer very closely. The original
planting holes were discovered, and part of the orchard
replanted with suitable varieties. At least, in part,
this success must be attributed to Jefferson's detailed
record-keeping and the thoroughness with which modern
American garden historians approached their task. We know
that by March 1811, Jefferson had more than 384 trees in the
south orchard, although, disasters in the form of frosts and

droughts often afflicted them, as he stoically recorded in his Garden Books. He planted Newtown Pippin and Esopus Spitzenburg apples, with Seckel one of his chosen pears.

FRUIT TREES AND ORCHARDS IN BRITAIN TODAY
After many years of decline, there are at last signs of a revival in orchards and fruit growing. It is still hard to run a successful commercial orchard in Britain, and especially an organic one. Demand from supermarket chains is directed to absolutely standardised, first-class fruit, without any blemishes (hard to meet in the climate), and capable of keeping a long time (some of the better-tasting varieties don't take to chilling in a gas-filled atmosphere during storage). Customers don't mind half as much as the supermarkets think: queues for local varieties of fruit at farmers' markets suggest that there is plenty of demand for non-standard products, and a fascination with interesting varieties of fruit. There is even a successful commercial quince orchard at Fingringhoe in rural Essex.

Very recently, awareness of orchards and their importance to the country as a whole has grown and been recognized by the government and in the media. Some government and lottery money is now becoming available to assist specific projects. The charity Common Ground has played an important part in trying to preserve and replant orchards, and has focused attention on what Britain stands to lose in terms of heritage, health and happiness if we cannot preserve traditional fruit varieties and smaller orchards. Its big success is the annual Apple Days it organises each autumn. The main vehicle of this fight back is the organic movement, and growing environmental concern about the extensive use of pesticides and sprays in commercial orchards, and the food miles associated with imports from distant countries. A simple desire for the best-tasting and most interesting fruit,

Right: Charles Trollope and his family have Britain's largest commercial quince orchard at Clay Barn Orchard, Fingringhoe in Essex. There has been a farm on the site since Anglo-Saxon times, and it is now expanding.

and an appreciation of the picturesque and aesthetic qualities of traditional orchards, have also motivated the movement. In 2007, the government added orchards to a priority list of endangered habitats, and a pilot orchard survey of nine counties has already identified some 13,000 orchards.

Many community-owned orchards, or those open to the public (for example, those belonging to the Royal Horticultural Society, the National Trust and stately homes), contain interesting fruit trees, often heritage varieties. Equally, there are some very distinguished private orchards, not generally open to the public – for example, Sir Roy Strong's famous garden at The Laskett near the Welsh border. The great fruit collections of the RHS are used as a teaching resource in its excellent educational courses. The collection of orchard trees at Brogdale in Kent (presently held in partnership with Reading University) is deservedly famous. All these serve to conserve stocks and heritage material, but we still need to grow them ourselves in our own gardens.

Most domestic gardens have been getting smaller as more and more land is built on. Fewer contain fruit trees, despite the development of smaller trees. People also move house more often, and are reluctant to plant trees that will only come to maturity for their successors. We love orchards (Samuel Palmer's painting *The Magic Apple Tree*, appeals to most of us at a deep emotional level), but we seem less keen to grow fruit ourselves, perhaps associating orchards more with romantic and picturesque decline than everyday use. The recent revival of interest in vegetable growing, as well as a general fascination with garden design, suggests this is due to change. We can all plant fruit trees in some form or other, wherever live.

Right: *The Magic Apple Tree* by Samuel Palmer shows an otherworldy vision of an apparently commonplace rural scene.

Orchard Fruit in
Garden Design

Take a moment to consider your ideal orchard. To some, it would be a pleasure garden; somewhere to walk or sit that is both beautiful and productive. An early 20th-century farmer's orchard would have had tall trees, with livestock grazing beneath. A cottager, of the same period, might have had a few small trees at the end of his garden, in amongst the flowers and vegetables, or as part of his hedge. Commercial orchards consist of symmetrical rows of low trees that are easy to pick. An orchard may have a few mixed trees, or many hundreds of the same. Trained fruit trees cannot, in any sense, be regarded as an orchard, but they are attractive and provide fruit, and can be useful additions to free-standing trees, or even an alternative if that is all you have room for. Equally, a single tree in a pot or a lone specimen on a lawn, does not constitute an orchard but they do bring many of the same benefits of beauty, restful shade and a harvest of fruit.

Unless you are growing fruit purely for commercial reasons, an orchard must surely be somewhere to sit in dappled shade and relax in surroundings that are both beautiful and productive. This can be achieved by planting a large orchard, but also by a few, well-placed trained trees as you want them. If you do not have room for an orchard, you can grow fruit trees amongst vegetables and fruit bushes, in an ornamental kitchen garden or amongst flowers in a border. The feel of an orchard is surprisingly easy to achieve, once you start planting fruit trees.

The most important consideration when designing any type of garden is to work with what you have. You cannot have a large orchard of tall trees if you have a small patio garden in a city, but equally, your garden will not be a success if you do not take into account its climate, soil and aspect. Working within your natural constraints will always be more successful than trying to fight them, and there are fruit trees for almost every site and soil. How to accommodate your trees' needs and ensure that they are pollinated is covered in 'Growing Fruit Trees'.

Rootstocks are also discussed fully in the same chapter, but their importance here is that, within reason, you can have both the variety and size of tree of your choice. Fruit trees are propagated by grafting varieties onto specific rootstocks, which will grow to a roughly predetermined size. Thus, you can have a fruit tree, regardless of how little space you have.

When planting fruit trees it is vital to give them enough space. The temptation will always be to put in an extra plant, but fruit trees do not appreciate being cheek by jowl. If air cannot circulate between the trees, you are more likely to suffer pests and diseases, and the trees will not flower and fruit so well. Leaving a little space between each tree will also give you a charming dappled effect beneath, rather than a dense canopy of shade.

Each of the fruit trees covered in this book is suitable for different sites, and will bring different benefits to your garden. A fruit tree will last for many years, so it is worth choosing carefully. You need to decide, possibly depending on the space you have, whether you want one type of fruit or a selection. If you have enough space for several trees, it is worth planting a mixture of fruits, then, if one has a bad year you will still have a harvest from the others.

APPLES

For many people apples are the quintessential orchard fruit. All but the smallest rootstocks, once mature, grow well surrounded by grass or meadow flowers, and those on dwarfing rootstocks can be grown in containers, or trained against a wall. In spring they have rich pink buds that open to dainty pink flowers, ranging from the palest shades through to brilliant candyfloss. The fruits ripen from summer through to winter, depending on the variety, and the trees are laden with fruits from the brightest reds to rich greens, with russet yellows and olive shades in between. As well as the look of

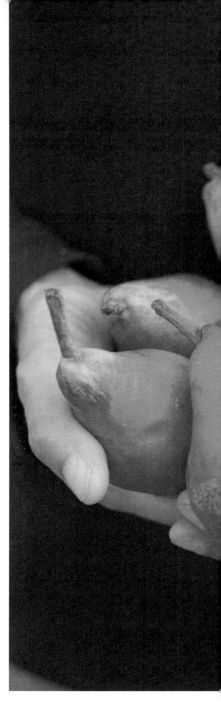

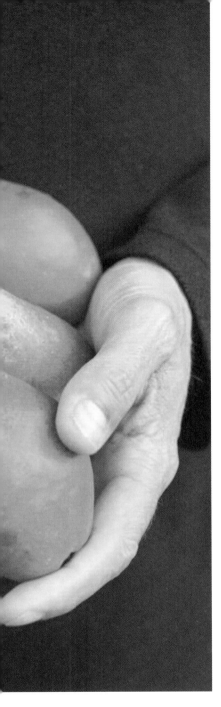

the tree, you need to decide the type of fruit you want. Dessert or cooking apples are the obvious choices, but don't forget cider apples, which grow into majestic trees. Crab apples grow into densely twiggy trees and produce small, prettily coloured fruits which are too tart to eat, but make wonderful jelly. They can be grown within hedges, and are useful pollinators.

PEARS

Pears have a slightly unfair reputation as being tricky to grow and slow to crop. These problems are largely overcome if you choose specimens grown on quince rootstocks, rather than their own. This will enable you to choose the size of the tree, and collect a harvest within a few years. The trees tend to be taller and thinner than apples, and the two grow well together in a mixed orchard. The beautiful greeny-white blossom comes early in the spring and can be at risk from frosts. Plant the trees in a sheltered spot, away from any frost pockets. Pears are one of the best trees to train against a wall, either as espaliers or fans. The warmth and protection of the wall will extend the geographical growing range, allowing you to grow the trees in colder regions than is normally possible. Another bonus is that the fruits hang down prettily off the horizontal branches. Pears dislike drought, and grow well in heavier soil than most other fruit trees will tolerate. As well as dessert pears, remember there are cooking pears or wardens, and perry pears that produce a fine drink.

PLUMS

These range from tall, upright trees to tangled, spiny shrubs. Plums, especially greengages, bear the earliest pure white blossom, which can look almost like snow. You can get dessert or cooking plums whose fruits range in colour from greeny-gold to rich velvety-purple. Greengages and mirabelles have smaller, rounder fruits that are pale green, with varying amounts of red streaking. Damsons tend to be more compact trees, with deep purple fruits. Finally, bullaces and sloes form little, twisted trees with small, blue-black fruits that ripen in late autumn. Beware of the last two, as they have vicious thorns. They are all reasonably happy in heavy soil, but need protection from frost, and do not like the competition of grass above their roots until they are well established. Greengages are delicate, requiring protection from wind and cold, whereas damsons and bullaces are tough trees, and can be used as windbreaks or planted within hedges.

CHERRIES

These are now available on a variety of rootstocks, which means that they can be grown to suit most spaces, and will thrive as trained fruit or in a container. The spectacular spring blossom can be pink or white, and, the fruits can be any colour from yellow to purply-black. Morello cherries are important, not only for their wonderfully sour cooking fruit, but also because – alone of all the fruit trees – they will thrive in shade or against north-facing walls. The blossom is not quite as amazing as that of dessert cherries, but it is still attractive. Morellos are also self-fertile, so if you have a tiny or shady garden, this is the tree for you.

QUINCES

Quinces grow into very pretty, twisted trees. They have one of the most beautiful blossoms in spring, with individual creamy-white or pink-tinged flowers like those of a wild rose. The fruits are also one of the most attractive, ripening to a rich golden yellow with a soft downy covering, and an almost overwhelmingly lovely scent. The blossom comes late and is therefore usually safe from frosts. Quinces can be grown in containers, but the twistiness of their branches means that they are hard to train into shapes against walls.

The quince that instantly springs to many people's minds is the flowering quince or *Chaenomeles,* rather than *Cydonia,* the true quince tree. These can be grown as bushes or trained as climbers, and are grown primarily as garden shrubs for their spring blossom, which comes in a huge range of colours from white to orange and scarlet to deep crimson. The fruits are not nearly as attractive as those of the true quince but they can be used to make jelly.

MEDLARS

If you want to grow a fruit tree that everyone will remark upon, grow a medlar. Their fruits earn them their quirky reputation, and, are more often grown for their appearance than their taste. They are olive-green and look like over-developed rose hips, or something much ruder, earning them their old English name of 'open-arse' or the French '*cul de chien*'. The trees are low-spreading and beautifully shaped with pure white blossom like dainty cups covering the branches in spring. In autumn the leaves turn rich shades of red and orange. This is the tree to choose for good winter appearance. No fruit tree looks unattractive, but the skeleton of a medlar can be truly beautiful. For this reason, they are particularly good specimen trees, although they will happily grow as part of a mixed orchard. The fruits make delicious jelly, but apart from a brief historical popularity, they have never really caught on for eating, so one or two trees would probably suffice.

MULBERRIES

There are two main mulberries; black and white. Unless you plan to breed silkworms, the white mulberry is best avoided as it is inclined to grow into a slightly boring upright shape and the fruits tend to be tasteless. The black mulberry is a wonderful tree with amazing fruit. The trees frequently lean to one side and develop an aged appearance very rapidly

Within a matter of years you will have a tree that looks as if it has grown in your garden for centuries. Their spreading branches eventually need support to prevent them from collapsing, but the forked wooden stakes – traditionally used for this – simply add to the charm of the tree. Like all fruit trees they lose their leaves in winter but, as with medlars, you are left with a wonderful shape. Mulberries need a sunny, sheltered site, but are more tolerant of pollution than other fruits. Grow them in the middle of a lawn where they can be seen to their best advantage, the fallen fruit will be easy to gather and the juice will do no harm. As the fruits ripen and fall, any surrounding paving will be stained a messy purple, as will you if you sit too long under the tree!

CHOOSING TREES

Having decided on the fruits you want, you then need to choose the right varieties for your garden. What to look for when buying trees is covered in 'Growing Fruit Trees', but there is more to a fruit tree than grafts and rootstocks. Part of the charm of all fruit trees is that they will rapidly become important characters in your garden, and it is worth choosing them carefully. Most will outlive you, and probably your children. There is much to be said in favour of choosing old varieties but more to be said in favour of local ones, many of which will have fascinating histories anyway. These will be the trees that will be happiest in your particular area. Varieties such as Stirling Castle and Tower of Glamis do particularly well in Scotland, while Greensleeves and Grenadier are more suited to Kent and Cornish Gilliflower and Cornish Aromatic to the West Country. Some old varieties may not crop so well, or be as resistant to disease. In the 19th- and early 20th-centuries, many orchards were heavily sprayed against pests and diseases, and some of these varieties may not do so well today if they are organically grown.

Look at orchards and gardens in your area to decide which varieties you like best, both in look and taste. There is no point growing a pear tree for its beautiful blossom if you do not also have a use for the fruits. In a large garden, a sea of blossom looks amazing; if you have room for only a few trees, try to stagger the flowering times so you have a longer season.

LARGE ORCHARDS

This section assumes that you have, within reason, unlimited space and can plan a large orchard of standard or half standard trees. Much depends on individual varieties, but as a rough guide a standard tree will have 1.8m (6ft) of trunk before the branches spread out, and will reach a final height and spread of about 5–6m (16–19ft). A half standard will have 1.4m (4ft) of trunk, and a maximum height and spread of about 4.5m (15ft). Before the development of dwarfing rootstocks, many orchards would have been grown on this scale, often with livestock grazing beneath. The spaces between the trees will depend on the varieties and rootstocks you have chosen. Equally spaced trees of a similar size will give your orchard a uniform feel, but there is no particular need for this approach. If you want to break it up, you can mix the fruits or alter the spacing, creating some wider paths or even glades amongst the trees.

Larger trees, surrounded by groups of smaller ones, will give you a number of different areas of interest within the orchard. You can even create a maze of paths between the trees, leading to an open centre, featuring a special tree such as a mulberry. As long as you leave enough space around the trees, it will be just as easy to harvest the fruit whether the varieties are all together or spread over the area. Do keep an accurate plan of which trees you plant where: they can be surprisingly hard to identify once they have grown up and lost their nursery labels.

Having planned the position of your trees, you need to decide what to have beneath them. Orchards of this size are usually best with grass, either grazed, mown or left as a wildflower meadow.

Animals grazing beneath the trees will give a lovely old-fashioned feel to your orchard, but you will need to look after the animals as well as the orchard! All livestock and poultry will keep the grass short and improve the fertility of the soil. Pigs (the Gloucester Old Spot pig is often referred to as the Orchard Pig), sheep and cows can also be happily kept in an orchard. Always provide protection, such as plastic tree guards or wooden 'cages', for young trees: cows may eat the leaves, and any animal may damage the trees by rubbing up against them.

Left: Keeping lifestock in your orchard – whether sheep, hens, geese or goats – will ensure that the grass beneath your trees is kept neat and tidy.

Right: A secluded corner in an orchard full of wild flowers is the perfect spot for a bee hive. The humble bee has a large role to play in pollination and could help your orchard to thrive.

Hens, ducks and geese kept in an orchard will earn their keep by eating insect pests, and giving you eggs. Ducks do not scratch as much as chickens and, therefore, do less damage but will need a pond to be truly happy. Geese are noisy and make brilliant guard 'dogs', but this may not be what you want in an orchard. They are also most likely to damage young trees.

Mown grass beneath the trees need not be kept particularly short unless you want a very pristine look. The grass beneath the trees is in dappled shade for much of the year, and will remain healthier if you allow it to grow slightly longer than a traditional lawn. Many of the prettiest orchards are those where the grass is allowed to become a sea of wildflowers. Bulbs, such as snowdrops, fritillaries, bluebells and scilla will provide a pretty carpet beneath the blossom, and daffodils look lovely in clumps around the trunks. Tulips can be geometrically planted to give a more formal feel. Traditional meadow flowers, such as poppies, campion, cornflowers and cranesbill geraniums then follow, lasting throughout the summer. These flowers encourage beneficial insects, especially bees that will help with pollination. Mown paths allow access through the meadow and make maintenance very easy. At first, it can be quite hard to achieve the correct balance of flowers and grasses but, once you have got this right, looking after a meadow is simple as you have to cut it only once a year in late summer or early autumn. A slightly unkempt feel will encourage wildlife in general into your orchard. Given a little encouragement birds, butterflies, badgers and bats will all visit and settle. Bat and bird boxes can be attached to the trees, and enclosing the orchard with mixed hedges is another way to extend the range of habitats.

Beehives are a worthwhile addition to an orchard: the hives look beautiful, while the bees pollinate the trees and provide you with honey. They are particularly easy to keep in a large orchard as you can position them in a relatively undisturbed area.

Orchards of large trees also make a wonderful children's play area. Swings and climbing frames can be incorporated, the trunks used as goalposts, and large apple trees are perfect for treehouses.

SMALL ORCHARDS

Obviously, everyone's idea of what is a small orchard varies, but here, we are assuming that you have room for somewhere between four and 20 medium-sized trees on semi-vigorous or semi-dwarfing rootstocks. The most important thing is not to overcrowd your trees. As with a large orchard, it is best to grow a mixture of fruits to give a longer season of interest, and safeguard against one crop having a bad year.

If possible, it is best to mix old and young trees – although this depends on there being some trees already in place when you plant your orchard. If you are renovating an old orchard, or adding to some existing trees, always leave some of the old

trees in place, even if they are not particularly productive. Trees on smaller rootstocks have a shorter lifespan than full-size trees, and staggering the ages of your trees will safeguard your orchard for the future. In a small orchard there is no particular merit in aiming at uniformity, which is only really effective on a grand scale. Trees of different ages will add interest to your orchard, and it won't matter if a tree does weaken and needs replacing.

If you don't have room for a traditional orchard, you can create much the same impression with a grove of fruit trees. At Penshurst Place in Kent, there is a long narrow avenue created by two rows of trees with a hedge on either side. It has the immediate feel of an orchard as you walk along the grass beneath the branches, even though it is only two trees wide. This may well have resulted from the spread of ideas from contemporary French garden design.

Whatever the size of your orchard, grass underfoot is an important element. Somewhere soft and sheltered to sit and picnic is vital, either on rugs beneath the trees, or seats in between. Remember that trees on semi-vigorous or semi-dwarfing rootstocks will start to spread their branches lower

Above: An avenue of fruit trees at Penshurst Place in Kent, England. Planting an avenue of trees lets you create the feel of an orchard even in a narrow space.
Right: White Triumphator and Queen of the Night tulips look stunning beneath spring blossom.

down the trunk, and benches or seats will need to be placed alongside the trees, rather than beneath them. Even if your orchard consists of only four trees, it is always worth having somewhere to sit and appreciate them – especially when there is dew on the grass, or for those who can't make it that far down!

Livestock is less practical on this scale, but hens or ducks could happily live in a little orchard, and wildflower meadows work well at any size.

Small orchards are often successful when they are not taken too seriously. You can add sculptures or even use the trees as sculptures, planting them in patterns or grid shapes. You can even do as the 20th-century garden designer, Russell Page, did and paint the trunks different colours. In hot countries, the stems of citrus trees are lime washed to deter insects and protect the thin bark from the direct heat of the sun, but you can use the same technique, ornamentally, using breathable paint. Lighting in a small orchard can be very effective, and practical if you want to eat there at night, but remember you want to cast gentle beams, not illuminate the entire area.

FRUIT TREES WITHIN A FLOWER GARDEN

In traditional cottage gardens there would have been no room
for an orchard, so the fruit was grown in amongst the flowers
and vegetables. Whether your garden is large or small, fruit
trees look lovely in flower beds and borders and usually crop
well because they have the same demands of sun, shelter and
well-drained soil as most garden flowers.

Small apple and cherry trees make good focal points in
a flower bed, giving height without creating dense shade, as
both are fairly open. Medlars and mulberries tend to cast too
dense a shade for much to grow well beneath them. You want
fairly small trees, but it is important that they start to branch
out well above the tallest flowers. Trees on dwarfing
rootstocks usually work well.

Quince trees and crab apples look good in hedges as their
twiggy growth complements the other hedge plants. You can
also use trained fruit to divide your garden, or as a backdrop
to long borders. If you use posts and wire as supports while
the trees are establishing their framework you can remove
them at a later date. This method of dividing a garden is very
useful as it takes up much less room than a hedge while also
being very beautiful.

Fruit trees provide a great deal of seasonal interest,
including blossom, fruit, some autumn colour and, depending
on your tree, spectacular sculptural shape in winter. You can
cut blossom for decoration (not too much!), eat the fruit and
use the wood for aromatic fires in winter. The attraction can
be extended by growing climbers through the trees. Vita
Sackville-West grew roses through her apples trees at
Sissinghurst in Kent. The important thing is to balance the
vigour of the climber to the size of the tree. Flame flower
(*Tropaeolum speciosum*) and sweet peas work well if they
are trained through smaller trees; larger trees can support
clematis and roses.

Tunnels of fruit trees look lovely, especially pears, as the fruit hangs down beneath the framework. At Bateman's, a National Trust property in Sussex, England, there is an alley of pears, including Doyenné du Comice and Conference, with flowering climbers planted in between. Shade-loving bergenia, lily of the valley, Solomon's seal and lungwort fill the beds at the base.

In new, large gardens, fruit trees are useful as they grow reasonably quickly and give an instant sense of history. The Dutch designer, Lodewijk Baljon, plants an orchard whenever he can, making the point that even a small orchard will give a garden a sense of rhythm. He is unusual amongst conceptualist designers in his use of plants, but he shows that orchards can be used in a very contemporary setting, not just as a nostalgic look back at tradition.

Fruit trees make good specimen plants, whether at the centre of a sweeping lawn, or in a small courtyard. Mulberries are the traditional lawn centrepieces, but a spreading medlar, a twisty quince, or an apple tree laden with rosy fruits would look just as good.

Above: The Dutch designer, Lodewijk Baljon, uses trained fruit trees in a striking and unusual way.

KITCHEN GARDENS

Free-standing fruit trees in a kitchen garden are a good way to grow fruit, and the trees give height and permanent structure to what can otherwise be a rather flat area. Peas and beans give temporary height, but a fruit tree is there throughout the year.

Ornamental kitchen gardens are created to look attractive, as well as being productive, and fruit trees are one of the most important elements in the balance. Examples can be seen at Audley End in Essex or Beningbrough in Yorkshire, England, or Domaine de Saint-Jean de Beauregard, Île de France – and, even in winter, these gardens look lovely.

Herbs are especially good partners for fruit trees. The herbs attract pollinating insects and, as they are usually cut rather than pulled up in the manner of annuals and many vegetables, the trees don't suffer root disturbance. Many herbs and flowers offer some natural help in the fight against pests and diseases. Some act as deterrents to the pests, while others provide a degree of protection against diseases. The most useful plants are given in 'Growing Fruit Trees'.

TRAINED FRUIT TREES

'A perpetual tapestry, covered in spring with flowers, in summer and autumn with fruit and foliage, beautiful even in winter with bare branches laced together in cunning artifice.' Trained fruit trees, as described by Antoine Le Gendre, the 17th-century French pioneer of fruit training, are a joy to grow. They can complement an orchard, be used in a kitchen or flower garden, and are a very useful and beautiful way of growing fruit in a restricted space. As already noted, growing trees against a wall also extends the geographical range where you can grow fruit. The supports themselves can also become a feature if you build a wall, rather than simply using a fence for instance, or posts and wires.

Crinkle crankle or zigzag walls that wind back and forth will give a better harvest as they have an increased surface area. They are also stronger structurally than a straight wall and they need only be one brick thick. Supports can also be posts, wires or fences, but these offer less protection.

Cordons consist of a single stem grown at a 45 degree angle which prevents too much apical (tip) growth, and encourages spurs all the way along the stem. This means that the tree will not grow too tall, and you will get fruit the whole length of the trunk. They need a constant framework of support and are not especially attractive, but they are the best shape if you want several varieties of fruit and only have a small space.

Espaliers are one of the hardest shapes to create, but also one of the most beautiful. They consist of a single, central trunk, with branches growing out horizontally at regular intervals. These trees need support to start with but, once the framework is established, they can become free-standing, creating an open boundary within your garden. Trees like this are almost fruit-bearing works of art, rather than mere trees. An even more elaborate shape is the palmette verrier, in which the branches are trained upwards at the end of each horizontal.

Fans are self-explanatory in shape, radiating outwards from a single central stem. They are not usually as sturdy as espaliers, but they provide the most efficient coverage of a wall, with branches and fruit filling every inch of space.

Step-overs are useful for lining paths or edging beds, where you do not want to create a tall barrier. When a single stem reaches 30–45cm (12–18in) in height, it is then trained horizontally. They are attractive because the fruit hangs down from the stem. Once the horizontal stem is firm, the support can be removed.

Minarettes are a single stem similar to a cordon, but, allowed to grow vertically. They do need constant pruning to prevent too much vertical growth at the expense of the productive side shoots.

Ballerinas are a similar shape to minarettes, but are bred so that they will maintain their shape without constant corrective pruning. After five years they will reach about 2.5m (8ft). They look attractive, both in flower and fruit, but they tend to be disease prone and the fruit quality is not brilliant. That said, they are constantly being improved with new breeding.

Within all these shapes there are a multitude of variations to suit any space. Cordons can be divided into two stems, and candelabras can be made with two or more stems rising from horizontals. All are useful, as they are relatively flat, taking up little space and looking extremely beautiful. But, like all strictly trained or modified plants, they do need constant care and

Opposite, clockwise from top left: Examples of trained fruit trees – cordon, espalier, step-over and fan.

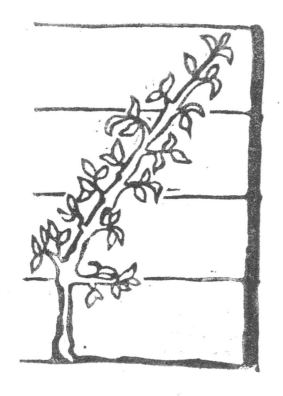

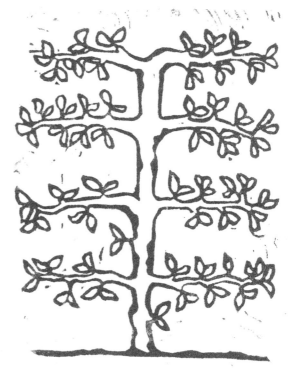

training if they are to remain healthy and looking their best. Freestanding trees can also be shaped. Pyramids consist of a wide circular base rising to a conical point. They are best grown up to 2.5m (8ft) and are a practical shape as well as being pretty as the maximum light reaches all the branches. Goblets were a shape that the Victorians copied from the French and are also suitable for small trees. In fact, many of the fancy shapes available were originally developed by the French, and even now two of the best places to see examples are the Palace of Versailles and the Luxembourg Gardens in Paris.

Family trees are a tree with two or more varieties grafted onto a single root. This means that they will pollinate themselves, and you can have a variety of fruit, including cookers and eaters. The problem used to be that one variety would dominate and you would end up with a lopsided tree but with improved breeding these are getting better all the time, and are invaluable if you want a variety of fruit but only have room for one tree. Minarettes are also available with different varieties one above the other.

FRUIT TREES IN CONTAINERS

Even if you have only a tiny space, you can enjoy some of the benefits of an orchard from a single tree in a pot. As long as you choose a suitable dwarfing rootstock, and a variety that isn't too rampant, almost any fruit tree can be grown in a container. You will still get fruit and the benefit of a tree. You can either allow the tree to grow naturally or train it into any of the above shapes. As long as you don't disturb the roots, you can also grow flowers and herbs around the base.

Right: A fan-shaped tree such as this morello cherry is both a practical and beautiful way of growing orchard fruits in a small space. The wall will provide protection and support, the spread fruits will receive the maximum sunlight and, even in winter, the bare branches will look attractive.

The Fruits

Apples

The Forbidden Fruit

'*A is for apple all shiny and red'*. It is entirely right, and not purely an alphabetical coincidence that the first entry on individual orchard fruits should be about the apple; for if you ask most people what fruit they associate with orchards, the answer will be 'apples'. Not only are they the most commonly grown orchard fruit in northern Europe but they also hold a central place in Western culture. They play important roles in biblical, classical and Celtic mythology, as well as making numerous appearances in literature, the visual arts, custom and ritual.

In Britain, the apple plays a vital role in cooking and, just as importantly, in a sense of national identity – it is still normal to refer to someone or something as being 'as English (or American!) as apple pie'. Many other nations may also have a fondness for the fruit, whether for French cider, Belgian fruit beers or German appefelstrudel. The qualities apples combine, range from innocence and perfection to sensuality and corruption, with more than a hint of spice, acidity and a certain amount of bitterness. Somehow, these are balanced in the roundness that appeals to the hand and touch, almost as much as to the tongue, the eye and our feelings about colour.

THE NAMING OF APPLES

Amongst the many reasons we love apples is their wonderful lexicon of names: these are particularly associated with the older varieties, even those that are hardly seen any more. Pippins, Costards, Catsheads, Codlins, Pearmains, Reinettes, Joanettings and Biffins, all evoke a rural arcadia and semi-magical world entered through the orchard – even if, as in most cases, the name actually results from a corruption or mispronunciation of French, or other foreign originals.

A Pippin is usually a small round apple derived from a seedling or pip (from the old Norman French *pepyn*), generally believed to have been imported into Britain from Normandy in the 1530s. Costards had arrived as early as 1292, and were sufficiently prized to command up to four times the general price for apples. Anyone who looks at a Catshead will see that it quite closely resembles its namesake. Codlins were named because they were coddled (cooked slowly) for eating. The Pearmain was, perhaps unsurprisingly, shaped rather like a pear. The word Reinette comes not from the French for 'little queen', but from the Latin *re natus* or born again, implying perhaps that the apple was a sport – or mutation – from an established variety. Even today, Orleans Reinette is one of the best tasting dessert apples. The word Joanetting, in fact, derives from the corruption of 'June eating', when such apples that are juicy, but not especially flavoursome nor long lasting, ripen. The Norfolk Biffin, traditionally baked slowly after the bread had left the oven, takes its name from the French *peau fin* or finely skinned!

Cider apples also look back to their rather earthy and rustic origins. Redstreak, Kingston Black, Foxwhelp and Slack ma Girdle are just a few names that seem to suggest a ruddy, energetic, rather unsophisticated and bucolic background. This may not be too far from the truth, given the periods of excess with which cider (sometimes substituted for part of an agricultural worker's wage until around 150 years ago) has been associated.

THE ORIGINS OF APPLES

Apples seem to have been around an awfully long time, although we still don't know quite how they got here. It is reasonably certain that their ancestors originated somewhere in, or near, present day Kazakhstan: the name of its capital, Almaty, can actually be translated as 'the City of the Apples'.

Until recently, it was thought that our present-day orchard apples (usually given the botanical name *Malus domestica*) arose via hybridisation between Asian apples and native wild or crab apples (*Malus sylvestris*). But recent publications suggest that our apples are, in fact, the direct descendants, without significant interbreeding, of those found in the Tien Shan mountains in central Asia, near Kazakhstan. Viable pips may have been carried in the guts of pack horses along the various trade routes from Asia to Europe, including the early lines of what is now the Silk Road, as long as 7,000 years ago. Such apples could have reached England and Ireland in pip form long before the Roman invasion of Britain. In the absence of archeological and manuscript evidence, proof of this theory largely relies on the techniques of DNA analysis: not easy to follow for a lay person. We can't help hoping such a romantic and wonderful theory will be vindicated!

Certainly, many European place names recall apples, either in the earlier, pre-Roman, Celtic 'Av', or the later old English 'aeppel'. For example, in France there are Aveluy and Havelu, in Spain Avila, and the legend of Avalon in Britain. Some French cider apples have ancient pre-Roman Breton names, such as Cheuro Ri Buhan.

APPLES IN ROMAN AND MEDIEVAL BRITAIN
It isn't clear whether apples were actively cultivated in Britain before the Romans invaded. We know they were eaten, and that Druids planted them as part of sacred groves, but we don't know whether these were wild or domesticated apples. In all probability, the Romans imported domestic apples and the skills of cultivating them, including grafting. After the fall of the Roman Empire, apples – often rather rough and used for cider making – appear to have survived, probably with difficulty, in monastic orchards.

The Norman Conquest supplied a boost to apple growing in Britain. Along with cider production it was established on a regular basis by the early 13th-century. The main cider apple seems to have been the Pearmain, in cultivation by 1204 when the Norfolk Manor of Runham had to pay taxes in kind that included four hogsheads of Pearmain cider. The Costard was

Right: Russetting has a most attractive effect on the colour and texture of many apples.

sold as an eating apple by 1296, and from this comes the word costermonger, in its original sense of an apple-seller. By the time of the Black Death, agriculture in general, and fruit and apple-growing in particular, was in decline. All the evidence suggests that things were in a very sorry way indeed towards the end of the 15th-century.

THE TUDORS AND STUARTS
Tudor peace and prosperity provided the stimulus and stable background needed for apple growing. During the 1530s, three things stimulated its rapid acceleration: a great increase in new high-quality fruit trees, a revival in demand led by royal consumption, and a good system of distribution in the form of merchants, fruit farmers and improved access to London. The catalyst for this growth was the royal fruiterer Richard

Harris – provider of fruit for the substantial appetites of Henry VIII and his court. He cultivated 105 acres of orchards near Teynham in Kent (still excellent fruit-growing country and close to the present day Brogdale fruit collection, see 'Gardens to Visit'). With royal encouragement, he systematically purchased grafts of the best French apple trees, concentrating especially on Pippins.

The result was a massive revival of the taste for, and consumption of, British apples that progressed remarkably steadily for perhaps 200 years. Many new varieties of apple were produced, and their taste and cooking potential was improved vastly. By 1629, John Parkinson was writing of around sixty carefully chosen favourite varieties. Some of his directions and comments on their cooking might well be worth a try today – for example, the Catshead (still an excellent cooking apple) could be stewed in rosewater, with sugar and cinnamon or ginger sprinkled over it.

Throughout 17th-century Europe, apples benefited from classification, recording and experimentation by connoisseurs who cooperated to swap varieties, or experiment with methods of training, improving or storing apples. It became easy to grow small, wall-trained apple trees on the famous Paradise rootstock, said to have originated in Armenia. Several French books about apple and fruit growing were translated into English, with the active participation of, gardener and writer, John Evelyn. In 1676, John Worlidge of Petersfield wrote *Vinetum Britannicum*, specifically on the subject of cider (the British wine of the title), providing valuable technical information.

APPLES IN THE 18TH- AND 19TH-CENTURIES
Many full-flavoured eating apples were bred in the 18th-century, often maturing and keeping well into autumn and even winter. Good examples of these still grown include

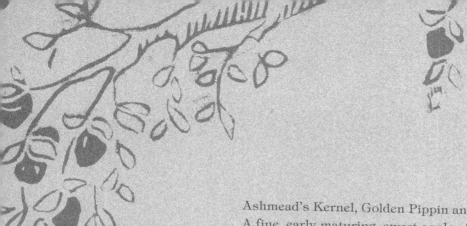
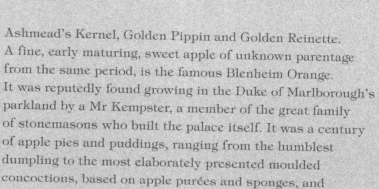

Ashmead's Kernel, Golden Pippin and Golden Reinette.
A fine, early maturing, sweet apple of unknown parentage
from the same period, is the famous Blenheim Orange.
It was reputedly found growing in the Duke of Marlborough's
parkland by a Mr Kempster, a member of the great family
of stonemasons who built the palace itself. It was a century
of apple pies and puddings, ranging from the humblest
dumpling to the most elaborately presented moulded
concoctions, based on apple purées and sponges, and
confectionery skills.

Very many of our best apples seem to have been produced
largely by chance, such as two deservedly long-loved
favourites, from the early 19th-century. Cox's Orange
Pippin was grown as a chance seedling of Ribston Pippin by
Mr Cox, a retired brewer. Its first fruit was produced in 1825.
Subsequently, it was promoted commercially on a massive
scale. The Bramley, of unknown parentage, was raised by
Miss Mary Anne Brailsford around 1810. Both eventually
took up the dominant positions in their category, which they
hold to this day. It is always a great delight to taste properly
tree-matured fruit from either of these varieties – infinitely
better than examples preserved in a fake environment, such
as a gas-filled cold store.

Juicy, crisp-skinned, early maturing apples from the
USA were imported during the 19th-century. Many had
been derived from the millions of pips saved in the pulp
(or pomace) left over from cider making, and then spread
on the vast acres of new land, as the country opened up to
settlers. The character of Johnny Appleseed, who spread
such pips on his travels throughout the USA, has entered
into American mythology as a symbol of growth in the new
land. In the cold climate of northern USA the pips germinated
well, and just a very few of the best-tasting proved worth
keeping and propagating for general use.

A few remarkable men had a huge influence on apple growing during the 19th-century. In particular, a Herefordshire landowner, Thomas Andrew Knight, did all he could to support his county's great cider-making tradition by publishing a remarkable series of colour plate illustrations of the most famous varieties. He also conducted serious research into fruit genetics, and was a little unlucky not to discover any underlying principles, that were subsequently exposed later in the century.

Later on, the nurseryman Thomas Rivers, also tested numerous new varieties of apple, which he obtained through his many contacts in the apple-growing world. Rivers, in turn, was great friends with the author Dr Robert Hogg who founded the Pomological Society in 1855, and wrote first-rate books on fruit growing. Hogg, along with the Reverend Charles Bulmer and Dr Henry Bull, helped drive the second revival of the Herefordshire cider industry in the 1870s. Together they were responsible for the publication of the *Herefordshire Pomona*, which described and illustrated the apples grown locally.

APPLE GROWING SINCE 1900

While apple orchards declined after the First World War, important scientific research was carried out at state-sponsored fruit research stations, such as Long Ashton in Somerset and Malling in Kent. This successfully tackled issues of disease resistance, keeping properties and marketability. As a result of their work, we now have good smaller rootstocks, so, we can grow apples in ordinary gardens without creating skyscrapers. We can preserve old varieties of apple and, just as importantly (using tissue culture and heat treatment), clean up the old material to rid it of long-running viral diseases to produce healthy new trees. Perhaps modern genetics could now combine really good flavour, reliable cropping and disease resistance to make commercial organic cultivation a less risky business.

Only recently has the apple revival really gained momentum, despite heroic efforts of individuals in the inter-war and post-war periods. Some of a large host of worthy names are: Julian Temperley, who has produced some of the finest small-scale cider apples in recent times; Sue Clifford and Angela King, the founders of Common Ground, which has done so much for the preservation of traditional orchards and fruit; and those great authorities on the apple, Dr Joan Morgan and Dr Barrie Juniper. There are thousands of others who deserve recognition, but no space to name them.

APPLES IN MYTHOLOGY, LITERATURE AND ART

In the West, apples are the subject of disproportionately more myths, rituals, sayings and representation in literature and art than any other fruit. You could say that this is something to do with the symbolic nature of the fruit itself, or simply argue that apples are the most common fruit and, therefore, feature so prominently. In China, for example, the peach takes the place of the less-well-regarded apple in many stories and images. There appears to be evidence of a sacred fruit tree in ancient Mesopotamian mythology many thousands of years ago, and this original construct influenced the development of classical, Celtic, Hebrew and Christian mythology.

Changes in the meaning of words over time make it remarkably uncertain exactly which fruits were referred to in classical myth and ancient history. For example a generalised Greek word, '*melon*', was used to refer to both apples and any round hard fruit. Many of the stories we assume to involve apples may, in fact, have referred to quinces, probably far more common in the early classical period. In one sense it doesn't matter: the myth is really concerned with profound human truths wrapped up in a story worth repeating.

In the West the story of Genesis takes the apple as the forbidden fruit in the creation myth (although the Hebrew word

concerned simply means fruit); while in the near and Middle East it is normally considered to be a fig (apple trees, need a long period of cold dormancy, and are unlikely to have been common in the region at that time). Masaccio's marvellous frescoes in Florence at Santa Maria del Carmine show what appears to be a fig tree, but Eve clutching something very like an apple in her hand. In 2008, Sir Anthony Caro sculpted *The Creation* for a bombed chapel near Dunkirk in northern France – his Eve figure appears to hold an apple.

The tension between creation and sex on the one hand, and death and oblivion on the other, is explicitly present in the story: God casts Adam and Eve out of Paradise *after* they have eaten from the Tree of Knowledge (the Apple) and understand the power of sex and creativity, but *before* they get a chance to eat from the also forbidden Tree of Life and 'live for ever'. In Christianity, the original tree of sin provides (in much accepted medieval interpretation) the material for the True Cross upon which Adam's descendent Jesus will die, and thereby redeem mankind. This is often alluded to by the presence of an apple, or very occasionally a quince, in Renaissance paintings of the Madonna and child, including many of exquisite sweetness by the Bellini family.

The same contrast between sexuality and death is implicit in the three major classical myths involving apples. Hercules risks death from a fearful monster to capture the golden apples of the Hesperides. When Paris is bribed, effectively with sex, to give the golden apple to the fairest of the three goddesses, his action precipitates the Trojan wars and the long years of slaughter. Atalanta, an exceptionally fast runner of semi-divine origins, can only be won in marriage by someone who can beat her in a race. Should they lose, they die. The victor, Hippomenes, distracts her by dropping exceptionally fine golden apples, or quinces, at crucial points in the race. In some variants of the myth, the subsequently united pair are overcome by lust and couple on the forbidden grounds of a temple: although they avoid death, for this sacrilege, they are turned into lions.

Celtic myth sees magic apple trees as the providers of life and energy, and is linked to the rebirth of life after midwinter. A greatly scaled-down version of this survives in the ceremony of wassailing the cider orchard, pouring libations of cider over the trees and firing guns to frighten evil spirits. Even now the ritual is still carried out in the West Country of England, and not purely for the benefit of the tourist board.

APPLES IN ART
Fine examples of paintings that include apples are Giuseppe Arcimboldo's *Autumn*, from his series of metamorphic *Seasons,* composed of fruit; and Chardin's solemn images

Right: Apple bobbing used to be a popular pastime at country fairs, the fruits being surprisingly hard to grip as they float in the water.

of fruit in a domestic setting, seeming to state nothing but still imply something infinitely beyond their humble surroundings. To Samuel Palmer, the apple tree (see page 49), set against a glowing world that is both the Kent countryside, somewhere infinitely stranger and otherworldly, is a symbol of all that is felt but not expressed. To Renoir, an apple was all colour, light and roundness; to Cezanne, the most wonderful way of exploring form; and to Magritte, who often used them in his works, a personal and unexplained symbol.

APPLES IN LITERATURE

References to apples are common in English literature from the Middle Ages onwards, sometimes used purely descriptively as part of the narrative, for example, the phrase *'Or hoord of apples leyd in hey or heeth'* in the *Millers's Tale*, from Chaucer's late 14th-century *Canterbury Tales*, which loosely translates as *'a store of apples laid (carefully) on hay or heather'*.

In the Elizabethan period they begin to reflect the huge range of new varieties introduced since the 1530s. Drayton's *Poly-Olbion,* his long narrative poem describing and praising England, sets out Kent and the Home Counties as a store of recently introduced and succulent varieties of apple, almost merging the place and its produce, as if the whole county were both the realisation of the mythical Hesperides, and a giant fruit tree producing mainly delicious apples.

> *Whose gentle Gardens seemeth Hesperides to mock;*
> *Nor them the damson wants, nor daintie Abricok*
> *Nor Pippin, which we hold of kernel fruits the King,*
> *The Apple-Orendge; then the savory Russetting:*

He goes on (at length) to name other apples common in his day: Peare-maine, Renat, Sweeting, Wilding, Costard and Pomewater. The poem, first published in 1612, but looks

Above: This is an original drawing, made by Beatrix Potter in 1905. It was reworked with cowslips for the publication of *Cecily Parsley's Nursery Rhymes,* as the publishers did not want a drawing of alcohol in a children's book!

backwards to Elizabeth's Golden England, is a wonderful symbol of the importance of apple growing in the period.

Shakespeare frequently mentions apples, choosing then common varieties appropriate to the setting and characters. In *Henry IV, Part 1,* the elderly Falstaff says: *'Why, my skin hangs about me like an old lady's loose gown; I am withered like an old apple-john.'* Apple-john is another name for the Juneating apple, which kept for a long time, but became very wrinkled as it got older. Pippins occur as a suitable end to a meal (*'There's pippins and cheese to come'* in *The Merry Wives of Windsor),* or as a special delicacy (in *Henry IV, Part 2,* Justice Shallow proudly says to Falstaff: *'we will eat a last year's pippin of my own griffin* [grafting], *with a dish of caraways',* demonstrating how central fruit growing had become to the English governing classes). One of Shakespeare's clowns is called Costard (*Love's Labours Lost*), and *The Taming of the Shrew* contains the saying: *'There's small choice in rotten apples.'*

Ever since reading Snow White, *I have
never quite trusted bright red apples.*
JANE

Half a century or more later, Marvell's poetry creates
a richly sensuous garden of the imagination where *'Ripe
apples drop about my head.'* In the romantic period, Keats'
Ode To Autumn of 1820 combines images of fruitfulness,
including apple trees and cider presses, and decay, with
a beautifully expressed feeling of melancholy.

Season of mists and mellow fruitfulness,
Close bosom-friend of the maturing sun;
Conspiring with him how to load and bless
With fruit the vines that round the thatch-eves run;
To bend with apples the moss'd cottage-trees,
And fill all fruit with ripeness to the core;

Robert Frost wrote of the sheer exhaustion and emotions
involved in harvesting fruit (to use the words of his epitaph
'I had a lover's quarrel with the world') in his poem, *After Apple
Picking*, first published in 1914, which included the lines:

And I keep hearing from the cellar bin,
The rumbling sound
Of load on load of apples coming in.
For I have had too much
Of apple-picking: I am overtired
Of the great harvest I myself desired.

APPLES IN POPULAR CULTURE

In many more general ways apples are embedded in our
culture, mythology and rituals. Everyone knows the story
of Newton, the falling apple (said to be a Beauty of Bath)
and the discovery of gravity – whether it is true is secondary.
In our own times the famous technology company's logo
implies a bite of the apple of knowledge, while the Beatles'
Apple Corps was a pun on the meanings of 'core' and

'corporation'. New York is generally referred to as the Big Apple, and several explanations for this are in common circulation. The apples in question are said to represent the fanciest girls in a famous New York brothel; or alternatively, that the horse-racing fraternity believed that the New York Races were the best rewarded or 'big apples'. By the 1920s, the Jazz Age musicians saw the city as the biggest and most important apple on the tree of possible locations, and spoke of 'playing the Big Apple'. By 1971, the name had become officially adopted by the tourist board to promote a positive image of New York.

CIDER, CALVADOS AND APPLEJACK

As everyone knows, apples can be fermented to produce an alcoholic drink – cider. This in turn can be concentrated by distillation to produce cider brandy (for example, calvados from Normandy, France). Freezing some of the water out of cider also raises the alcoholic strength to produce applejack. This was originally a frontier or backwoodsman's drink in the USA and Canada, but is now popular for making the most delicious sorbets. All three can be used in cooking, especially for sauces with pork, game (including pheasant and rabbit) and fish. Additionally, the flaming spirits make a spectacular display poured over fruit.

Cider manufacture has been established for centuries and played a significant part in the planting of monastic orchards in northern France and Britain. Cider, and its end products, are generally made using specific apples with high concentrations of tannin and acids, and bear some wonderful names. The old cider orchards of Hereford, with tall standard trees planted far apart, are a significant part of Britain's imaginative heritage, even if nowadays only artisan producers rely fully on locally grown crops and traditional methods of manufacture.

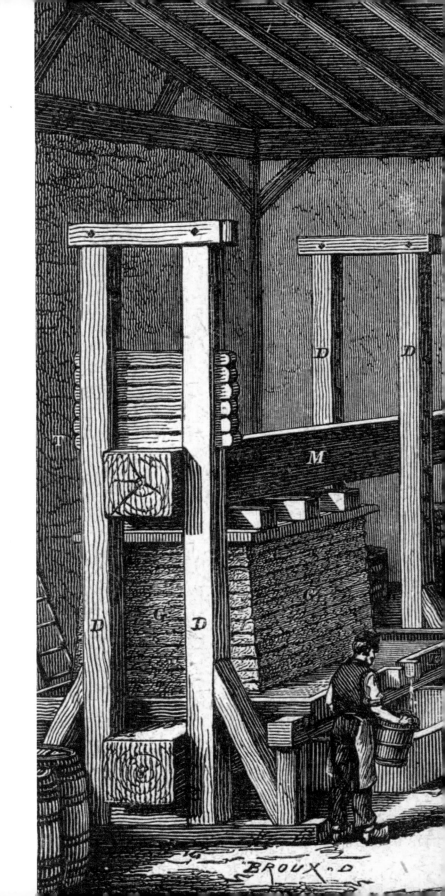

Right: Late 19th-century cider production in France. Although artisan in scale, this is a highly efficient system with the horse providing all the labour.

EATING AND COOKING APPLES

Of all the orchard fruits, the apple is the most versatile and most loved in the kitchen and at the table. The best eating apples have been discussed in terms that might make you think they were the finest wines. Edward A. Bunyard in his *Anatomy of Dessert,* published in 1929, describes Blenheim Orange as '*having a mellow austerity as of a great port in its prime*'. The balance of sugar, acidity and tannins, along with the texture of flesh and skin, all influence the experience of eating a really special dessert apple. The different flavours that you may be able to detect are wide ranging.

What you taste in an apple is obviously hugely subjective and personal. One of the greatest authorities on apples, Joan Morgan, has compiled a list of flavours associated with particular varieties. Some of them included wine (McIntosh), strawberries (Worcester Pearmain), raspberries (Reinette Rouge Etoilée), honey (Crispin), aniseed (Ellison's Orange), nuts

(Blenheim Orange) and pineapples (Pine Apple Russet and Ananas Reinette). Try them to see if you agree, perhaps at one of the many Apple Days that take place countrywide every autumn.

Cooking apples (a definition unique to Britain) often have relatively high concentrations of acids and pectin, and often fluff up when cooked. Cooking apples offset the body of pork or the strong flavour of game, and also provide a foil for sugars, pastry cases and crumble mixtures. A really good, properly matured, Bramley is far better than the usual supermarket clone. Catshead and Newton Wonder are also excellent if you can find them. Some eating apples also work remarkably well: for example, Russets and Pippins in a tart.

The classic dishes below never disappoint; you can ring the changes with different apple varieties and flavourings. They are a starting point not a substitute for your own prized family recipe. If you use the best-quality ingredients that you can afford, your reward will be in the results.

Apple Recipes

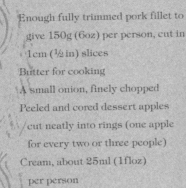

Enough fully trimmed pork fillet to
 give 150g (6oz) per person, cut in
 1cm (½ in) slices
Butter for cooking
A small onion, finely chopped
Peeled and cored dessert apples
 cut neatly into rings (one apple
 for every two or three people)
Cream, about 25ml (1floz)
 per person
Good chicken stock, cider
 or Calavados

Serves 4 to 6
450g (1lb) cooking apples, peeled,
 cored and sliced
1–2 tablespoons sugar
about 40g (1½ oz) butter

Pork with Cream & Apples

This excellent dish is good enough to serve at a supper party, and is easily prepared. You just need to make sure that the pork is completely trimmed (the butcher will do this, if asked nicely) and the apples look much better in neat rings or segments. This works best with dessert apples – Russets are good.

Cook the onion in butter until soft, but not brown, and reserve it. Cook the apple rings separately in butter until golden brown, but not mushy; set aside. Cook the pork gently in a little butter over a medium heat: if you cook it too fiercely, it may become dry and hard. Lift out and reserve. Deglaze the pan, using whatever liquid you have decided upon, and reduce the resulting liquid. Thicken the sauce with the cream, and return the pork to finish cooking. Arrange neatly on individual plates, garnished with the warm apple rings.

Bramley Apple Sauce

Apple sauce is hard to beat with roast pork or duck. If you don't have Bramleys to hand, you can use other types of cooking apple. The exact quantities depend on the tartness of the apples and personal taste – those given here are a good starting point.

In a small pan, cook the apples with just enough water (2–4 tablespoons) to stop them sticking or burning. Then add the sugar and the butter. When the apples are soft, beat the sauce or fluff it up with a fork. You can add a piece of lemon peel, cloves or cinnamon but it is generally best kept simple.

Apple Pie

Serves 6

225g (8oz) flour

115g (4oz) unsalted butter,
   chilled and diced

Salt

1.5kg (3lb) cooking apples

Lemon peel, cloves or cinnamon
   (optional)

115g (4oz) granulated sugar and
   some to sprinkle on top

Beaten egg or egg white to glaze
   (optional)

Apple pie is an iconic dish and a traditional great puddings. At its simplest, you can make it very quickly, and quite well, using chilled supermarket shortcrust pastry on top of a dish of chopped apples with sugar. The variations are considerable; flavourings (grated lemon peel, cinnamon and cloves are the most usual) and homemade pastry are the beginning. Catsheads or Newton Wonders substitute well for the traditional Bramleys, or Pippins, if you can find them in a farmers' market. On the top you can certainly go in for pastry decorations and glazes. But whatever you do, make it! This recipe will serve six easily, and is based on simple homemade shortcrust pastry. Serve with thick cream.

Pre-heat the oven to 200°C/400°F/Gas 6. Make the pastry by hand or in a food processor. In either case, add the diced chilled butter and a little salt to the flour, mixing as appropriate until the mixture forms fine breadcrumbs. Add enough cold water to make it easy to knead the mixture into dough. Form it into a ball, wrap in foil, and refrigerate for half an hour.

Roughly chop the peeled and cored apples, place in a pie dish so that they come fairly near the top. Mix in the sugar, a little water and any flavourings.

Roll out the chilled pastry to a size a bit bigger than the dish, drape it around a rolling pin and place it on top, pushing down the rim and marking it with a fork if you want. At this stage you can apply decorations or just leave it plain. Glaze it with beaten egg or egg white, if you like – it will look nicer, but this is not essential. Finally, sprinkle with a little sugar and put it in the preheated oven. It will need about 20 minutes at 200°C/400°C/Gas 6, followed by another 15 minutes, with the temperature reduced to 180°C/350°F/Gas 4, by which time the pastry should be golden and crisp.

Serves 6

260g (9oz) flour

150g (6oz) butter, chilled and cubed

75g (3oz) sugar for crumble

450g (1lb) cooking apples, peeled, cored and sliced

50g (2oz) sugar for apple mixture

Apple Crumble

Crumbles are one of the supreme puddings for a cold day. They go well served with real custard, cream or ice-cream. They are infinitely flexible in terms of ingredients, and reheat well. Blackberry and apple, plums and many other orchard fruits all work well. You can use flavourings at your discretion: cinnamon and cloves for apple, vanilla for pears, and almond for plums and damsons. The topping has endless possibilities. You need approximately equal weights of flour (substitute ground nuts such as almonds, or rolled oats, for some of the flour, if you want) and of a butter and sugar mix (use approximately twice as much butter as sugar, which can be of any type).

Preheat the oven to 190°C/375°F/Gas 5. To make the topping, place the flour in a bowl along with the slightly chilled, cubed butter. Mix with your fingertips to an even texture of fairly small crumbs. Mix in 75g (3oz) sugar.

In a saucepan, slightly precook the peeled, cored and sliced apple with the remaining sugar and 1 tablespoon water for about 5 minutes; tip it into your dish, and then cover with the crumble mixture and place in the oven. It will take at least 20 minutes to cook, and the topping needs to be golden, or rather darker, if you prefer.

Alice Soubranne's Recipe for Tarte aux Pommes à l'Alsacienne

This recipe comes through a long history of family exchanges between the Kelly and Soubranne families, and was kindly cooked on several occasions by Alice on a recent visit to England. It is as French as the apple pie is English, and quite delicious. With this recipe presentation is important, with evenly cut apple rings and golden custard. Quantities of pastry and

apples are determined by the size of the flan dish and apples themselves, while the size of the egg yolks determines the precise quantities of the other custard ingredients. Good apples for this recipe should have a slightly spicy taste with plenty of acidity, and hold their texture when cooked in the custard. Norfolk Pippins, Ashmead's Kernel's and most Russets are ideal. Of the generally available supermarket apples, Braeburn is reliable and tastes good, holding enough texture. Bramleys are too tart.

Blind bake the pastry in a 25 cm/10in buttered flan case with removable base at low temperature (approx. 180°C/350°F/Gas 4). The shell should be firm and dry, but not browned or biscuit like. Cut the peeled and cored apples into even slices, arrange prettily in concentric circles on the pastry and bake at approximately 180°C/350°F/Gas 4 until softened but holding their shape (say 10 minutes).

In a big bowl, beat the egg yolks with the sugar; the mixture should be neither too sweet nor solid. Then fold in the gently melted butter and crème fraîche, and pour this custard mixture over the apples in the flan dish.

Cook the tarte for 30 minutes in a hotter oven (approx. 190°C/375°F/Gas 5) so it is, in Alice's words, 'goldy and has a tan' but does not burn. It must not turn dark brown or the custard will curdle at the edges, making a break line where it meets the pastry. Eat cold, served with crème fraîche or cream.

Other fruits can, in principle, be used for this tarte, including plums and cherries, but it's important to get the right liquid content and height in relation to the finished custard.

See also, Apple and Cinnamon Cake, page 129

Serves 4 to 8, but we recommend not sharing with anyone
Sweet pastry, use pâte sucrée or
  a standard block of chilled
  supermarket pastry
3–4 apples
6 egg yolks
4–5 tablespoons caster sugar,
  approx. 90g (3½oz)
55g (2oz) butter, melted
500ml (1 pint) crème fraîche

Pears

The Fruit of Perfection

Pears are undoubtedly the aristocrats of the orchard. Tricky to grow, delicate and perishable, they are only at the peak of perfection for a short time. These very difficulties led to their enhancement, and for those who took the trouble there were the rewards of almost perfect fruit. A ripe pear stood for elegance and grace, the voluptuous form of a woman, the promise of perfection in both looks and taste. The Ancient Greeks compared them to the fleeting beauty of youth, and later breeders called them after kings, queens and emperors.

THE HISTORY OF PEARS

Pears originated in central Asia, and spread along the ancient trade routes erratically, as the trees do not grow true from seed. The ancient Phoenicians, Greeks and Romans grew them, with the two latter civilisations developing successful breeding programmes. Cato described growing techniques in his book, *On Agriculture.* He recommended *Aniciana sementiva,* which was probably a late-ripening variety eaten at Sementiva, the Roman early winter festival, to celebrate the end of sowing and *Volaema,* so called because it fitted into the palm of the hand (*vola*) when picked. Pliny the Elder recommended *Crustumian* for flavour and *Falernian* for juices and wine. There is no definite evidence that the Romans brought pears to Britain, but by the time of the Battle of Hastings in 1066, they were very popular in France, and the invading Normans would certainly have brought over their favourite varieties. By the time of the Domesday Book in 1086, pears were specifically mentioned as boundary markers.

Pears at this time were gritty and needed to be cooked before they became palatable. The most famous pears were Wardens, which may have been raised in the 14th-century by the Cistercian

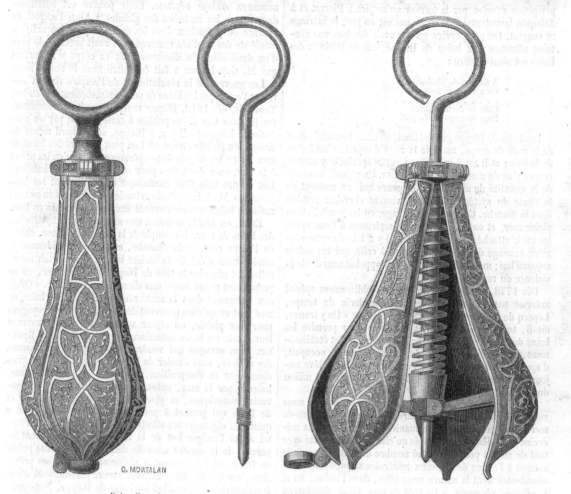

Poire d'angoisse. — Musée du Louvre ; collection Sauvageot. — Dessin de Montalan.

Above: The *poire d'angoisse* or pear of anguish was a particularly nasty instrument of torture.

monks at Warden Abbey in Bedfordshire. Very large and extremely hard, they were often regarded as a separate fruit in their own right. They needed to be cooked slowly to be edible but were one of the few fruits that could be stored right through winter. In Shakespeare's *A Winter's Tale,* a Warden pie, coloured with saffron, is made for the shepherds' feast. Black Worcester may have been one of the original varieties. The fruit was used as a crest by the Worcestershire bowman in the Battle of Agincourt in 1415, and has appeared on the town's coat of arms since the reign of Elizabeth I.

A less pleasant association from the Middle Ages is the *poire d'angoisse* or pear of anguish; a particularly nasty instrument of torture used on heretics, homosexuals, witches and women who had miscarried and were regarded as evil. It consisted of four iron 'leaves' hinged together in the shape of a pear with a spring mechanism or screw in the centre. It was inserted into an orifice to match the crime, and sprung or screwed open. The victim rarely died from the torture itself, but as the instruments were never washed they would almost certainly have died from the resulting infection. Many were elaborately decorated with pictures of Satan, and appear to be beautiful objects until you understand their purpose!

In the 17th- and 18th-centuries pear breeding really took off, with France leading the way. Louis XIV of France was a keen fruit grower and pears were one of his favourite fruits. There is even a variety called Ah Mon Dieu, which is said to commemorate his exclamation on first tasting a pear. (More prosaically, it may have originated at the Chartreuse de Mon-Dieu in the Ardennes.) One of Louis' pastimes was to peel a pear in such a way that the skin could be put back in place and presented to a courtier. His fruit gardener, or *Intendant général des jardins fruitiers et potagers de toutes les maisons royales*, was Jean-Baptiste de la Quintinie. He developed the system of espaliering, which gave the delicate pears the protection they needed to thrive. This meant that they could be grown around Paris, thus reaching wider markets. In the days before railways and good roads, fresh food could really only travel about 20 miles (32km) to market by cart. De la Quintinie wrote a gardening manual in 1690 in six volumes, which was translated into English by John Evelyn. He praised pears above all other fruits, describing over 500 varieties, compared with only 27 apples – which he justified with the damning remark '*there is no great difference among them in goodnesss*'. Britain followed slowly but even here pears were the most highly prized fruit, with 64 varieties in 1640 and more than 700 by 1842.

The 18th-century *Encyclopédie* of Diderot and d'Alembert also praised pears, saying that they were grown in the gardens of the wealthy, whereas apples were found in the orchards of common people. This may sound like terrible snobbery

but the logic was simply that apples were easier to grow and stored better. Pears also reached the kitchens of the rich and famous. In the late 19th-century, ladies in France began to dine out – previously only those of questionable virtue had been seen in restaurants. It was important to flatter these new diners so, Escoffier, the great chef of the moment, created a series of dishes to tempt them. *Poires Belle-Helene* was created for Gabrielle Réjane, the star of Offenbach's opera of the same name.

FAMOUS PEARS

Most of the best-known pears date from the 19th-century when breeding reached its height. Williams' Bon Chrétien or Bartlett, as it is known in the USA, has a distinguished history, and is still one of the best varieties of pear available today. The original Bon Chrétien pear was brought to France from Calabria, and may have been the Roman variety *Crustumian* or *Volaema*. In the 15th-century, Louis XI summoned Saint François de Paul from Calabria, in the hope that the saint's prayers would improve his health and give him everlasting life. This was not possible, but Saint François' piety was such that he earned the name Good Christian at court. The pears that he had brought with him, and loved so much, earned the same name. In 1770 a seedling appeared in the garden of a schoolmaster called Wheeler, and, grew into a particularly fine tree. His successor, John Stair, took grafts and sent them to the nurseryman, Richard Williams. The pears bore a resemblance to the ancient variety and became known as Williams' Bon Chrétien, although locally they retained the name Stair's Pear. In 1817 plants were sent to the USA where they ended up at the nursery of Enoch Bartlett, without their labels. He recognised the worth of the fruit and named them Bartlett. By the time the mistake was uncovered it was too late to do anything. They were used in the Californian canning industry, and are now the most widely grown pear in the world.

Doyenné du Comice is, for many people, the ideal pear: even its name, 'top of the show' implies perfection. Pear breeding had increasingly been moving away from the hard, gritty fruits of the Middle Ages towards the smooth, buttery texture we prize today. Bunyard, in his *Anatomy of Dessert* wrote: '*Here at last was the ideal realised, that perfect combination of flavour, aroma and texture of which man had long dreamed.*' He went on to lament that he had not been alive at the time to taste the first fruits and pitied the earlier gourmets, such as Brillat-Savarin, who had missed it altogether. It was raised in 1849–50 by the typical French partnership between an aristocrat with money and enthusiasm, and a skilled gardener, who did the work. The financier was Millet de la Turtaudiere, President of the Comice Horticole and the gardener was Dhommé. Sadly, the garden no longer exists but they are celebrated by a plaque at the site in Angers, interestingly crediting the gardener first.

Conference, one of the last of the great 19th-century pears, was raised by Thomas Rivers in 1885. Its name commemorates the National Pear Conference, which the Royal Horticultural Society held at Chiswick, in London, that year. Raised from seed it is a truly wonderful pear!

PEARS IN LITERATURE

Pears have made appearances in literature throughout history, sometimes fleetingly simply as themselves, often with subtle double meanings.

Both Boccaccio and Chaucer used pear trees as a means of hiding lovers from husbands. Boccaccio's *Decameron* was written in 1349, and in one of the tales, Lydia, married to the elderly nobleman Nicostratos, falls hopelessly in love with her husband's servant, Pyrrhus. He sets her three tasks to prove she really is in love with him, and not just testing his loyalty to Nicostratos. Lydia replies that not only will she complete the three tasks, but also will make love to Pyrrhus in full view

of Nicostratos, persuading her husband that he is suffering from hallucinations. This is where the pear tree enters the story, their hallucinatory effects already well-known from French fables. Pyrrhus climbs the pear tree to pick fruit for Lydia, but pretends to be shocked at the sight of a couple making love below. Disbelieving Pyrrhus, Nicostratos climbs the tree and, inevitably, sees Pyrrhus and Lydia making love. By the time he descends they are sitting side by side, denying everything. Lydia insists that the poor pear tree is cut down for besmirching her honour with its hallucinations.

In Chaucer's *Merchant's Tale* there is a similar love triangle, with May married to the elderly and blind January, but with the servant, Damyon, as the instigator. He climbs into a pear tree and May climbs onto her husband's shoulders to pick '*smale peres grene*'. The inevitable ensues, and at the crucial moment January recovers his sight. May manages to persuade January that her '*struggle with a man upon a tree*' was exactly what cured his blindness, and in this instance the tree is saved.

The pear at the beginning of Tolstoy's *Anna Karenina* may just be a pear, or, may again have deeper meaning. Oblonsky brings it home for his wife, and it may simply be that pears were prized at the time in Russia, but, equally, in Russian folklore pears were associated with masculinity, and this is a man who has been having an affair with the French governess and is about to be confronted by his wife!

Pears stand for many other things in literature, and in Dickens' *David Copperfield,* Uriah Heep compares his intention to marry Agnes Wakefield with the picking of an unripe pear. David observes, '*he made motions with his mouth as if the pear were ripe already and he were smacking his lips over it*'.

R. D. Blackmore, the author of *Lorna Doone,* adopted a more practical approach and became a market gardener, breeding pears and other fruits on a 12-acre-site at Teddington in West London. He actually resented the fame *Lorna Doone* brought him, and was more proud of his career as a gardener and writer of articles on fruit. Unfortunately, he had little business sense and out of forty years breeding fruit he made a profit in merely two.

PEARS IN LANGUAGE

'Apples and pears' is a well-known Cockney expression for stairs. It has no hidden meaning: it was the rhyme that was important. Developed so that the Cockneys of the East End of London could converse in a type of code in front of the police, the rhyming slang transforms ordinary sentences into meaningless gibberish.

'Pear-shaped' is a common expression in Britain and Australia, originally referring to shape, flattering or otherwise, depending on the context. In the 20th-century it increasingly came to mean that something that had gone awry. This may have originated in the Royal Air Force when acrobatic loops which went wrong became pear-shaped instead of round. Whatever the origin, it is less well known in the USA, and caused consternation when Margaret Thatcher used it in a speech to Ronald Regan on her first visit there!

DRINKS AND OTHER USES

Perry is a drink similar to cider. It was spread across much of Europe by the Romans, and was later produced on a large scale by the Normans. It remained popular in France but in Britain it largely disappeared during Victorian times and fell into obscurity until its reinvention as Babycham in the 20th-century.

The name first referred to wild pear trees and was later used for the drink made from their fruit. Perry (and cider) were regarded as healthy drinks, rather than intoxicating alcohol, and William Lawson in his *A New Orchard and Garden* of 1618 wrote: '*These drinks are very wholesome, they coole, purge and prevent hot agues.*' John Gerard, the herbalist, writing in 1597, had been slightly more cautious, warning that it *'purgeth those that are not accustomed to drink thereof'*. The charming names of perry pears also carried a warning: Merrylegs and Mumblehead being two.

Perry is fizzier than cider, and in Georgian London it was frequently marketed as champagne. By the end of the 19th-century, though, perry production was largely restricted to Devon and the area around Gloucester, Hereford and Worcester, with the finest vintages coming from within sight of May Hill in Gloucestershire. After the Second World War it received an unexpected boost when the Showering family of Shepton Mallet exhibited a sparkling perry at the local agricultural show. It was nicknamed the Baby Champion and later became Babycham. Unfortunately, thanks to the advertising campaign, many people were led to believe that it was produced by a magical fawn rather than from simple crushed pears.

Eau de vie can be flavoured with a whole pear in the bottle. Like traditional ships in bottles the great question is: how does the pear fit down the narrow neck? The method is actually very simple; a pear is chosen while still tiny and a bottle is fitted over the fruit, being taped to the branch to keep it in place and stop insects getting in. Once it reaches full size the pear is cut from the tree and the spirit added, producing an attractive and delicately flavoured drink. This might be something that you would like to try in your own orchard, or on your favourite fruit tree. If you do, make sure that the bottle is securely fixed in place and will not fall as the pear gets larger and heavier.

As well as the fruit, the wood and bark of pear trees can be used. The bark produces an attractive yellow dye and also contains arbutin, an antibiotic. The wood itself is hard and excellent for carving. It is also used for smoking foods, giving them a delicate flavour.

EATING AND COOKING PEARS

Attempting to describe the pleasure of eating a pear can lead to literary excesses. Edward Bunyard in the *Anatomy of Dessert* of 1929 starts: '*I begin with a confession. After thirty years of tasting Pears I am still unfurnished with a vocabulary to describe their flavour.*' However this does not stop him and he goes on to talk about texture: '*As it is, in my view, the duty of an apple to be crisp and crunchable, a pear should have such a texture as leads to silent contemplation.*' And he is not alone, an unknown, but 'cultured French gourmet' is quoted in the same book: '*To savour a pear, a cultivated and exercised palate is necessary to appreciate and separate the subtle flavours.*' You can see why the commoners stuck to growing apples!

Depending on the variety, pears can be eaten raw or cooked. Their flavour is complemented by red wine, almonds and vanilla, and they go well with cheese or chocolate. The recipes overleaf will give you some idea of their versatility.

Right: Many orchard fruits, such as these Conference pears, have wonderful shapes and colours that they make natural subjects for the decorative arts and pattern makers.

The trees in our orchard doubled up as supports for the washing line and goalposts for football, but in theory, not at the same time.

JANE

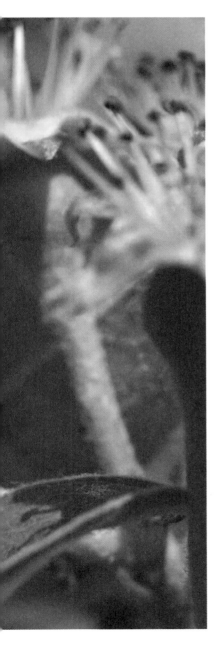

Pear Recipes

Serves 4 as a starter, 2 as a light meal
2 pears, ideally Williams' Bon
   Chrétien or Doyenné du Comice
50–110g (2–4oz) goats' cheese or
   blue cheese
110–200g (4–7oz) watercress,
   spinach or rocket, washed
   and dried
50g (2oz) walnuts or hazelnuts
Nutty bread, to serve
For the dressing:
3 tablespoons walnut or hazelnut oil
1 tablespoon lemon juice
Seasoning

Pear and Cheese Salad

Everything depends on the quality of the ingredients: sweet juicy pears, sharp creamy cheese, peppery salad leaves and the crunch of nuts.

Make the dressing. Core and slice pears. Coat with dressing immediately to stop them turning brown. Crumble or slice cheese. Toss leaves in dressing. Arrange leaves, pears and cheese on a plate. Scatter nuts on top.

Pear and Almond Tart

This is a very pretty tart, with the glossy pears gently rising above the almond mixture. It is also extremely easy!

Serves 4 to 6

100g (3½ oz) unsalted butter, soft

100g (3½ oz) caster sugar

½ teaspoon natural almond essence

2 large eggs, lightly beaten

30g (1¼ oz) plain flour

100g (3½ oz) ground almonds

3 or 4 pears, just ripe, Conference are good.

1 tablespoon lemon juice

2 teaspoons apple or quince jelly

Tart tin 23cm (9in), lined with shortcrust pastry, and blind baked

Pre-heat the oven to 200°C/400°F/Gas 6. Beat the butter, sugar and almond essence together.

Add the eggs, flour and almonds, mix gently and pour into the pastry case. Peel, halve and core the pears, and brush them with lemon juice to stop them turning brown. Arrange the pears cut side down on top of the filling. Bake for 30 minutes.

Mix the jelly with a little warm water so it will spread easily. Remove the tart from the oven and brush over with the glaze. Return to the oven for about another 10-20 minutes, until the top is golden and a skewer comes out cleanly. Leave to cool and serve with lots of thick or clotted cream

Adam and Eve's Pudding

This was named by the husband of one of our recipe testers, Charles Kerr. It has nothing to do with the Garden of Eden, but the recipe is for pears and, as he says, Adam and Eve were a 'right pair!' It is best using firm pears such as Conference, which will hold their shape in the toffee and contrast with the sponge on top. Depending on the greed of your guests, you may need to double the quantity of toffee to use as accompanying sauce.

Serves 4 to 6

800g (1lb 12oz) pears (about 6 or 7), peeled, cored and cut into chunks

25g (1oz) unsalted butter

For the sponge:

110g (4oz) self-raising flour

1 teaspoon baking powder

110g (4oz) unsalted butter, soft

110g (4oz) caster sugar

2 large eggs

1 teaspoon vanilla extract

For the toffee:

1 dessertspoon golden syrup

110g (4oz) light brown sugar

50g (2oz) unsalted butter

100ml (3½ floz) single cream

1 teaspoon vanilla extract

Preheat the oven to 180°C/350°F/Gas 4. Put the toffee ingredients into a small saucepan, heat slowly while they mix, and then boil for 3-4 minutes.

Melt the butter in a large saucepan, and add the pears. Heat until they begin to soften, and add enough toffee sauce to cover them (about half). Continue until the pears are almost cooked. Pour into a 1½ litre (2½ pint) pie dish and leave to cool a bit.

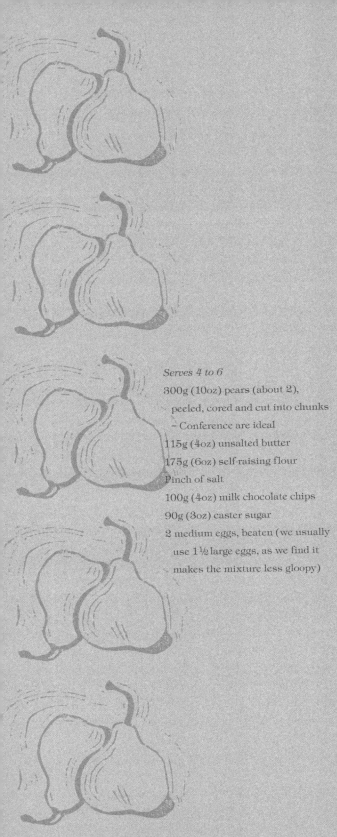

Sift the flour and baking powder into a large bowl. Add the other ingredients. Mix roughly with a fork so that the flour doesn't fly everywhere, and then mix with an electric hand-whisk. You can use a food processor, but the sponge may not rise so well as you won't get as much air into the mixture. Add 1 or 2 tablespoons of warm water so that the mixture plops off a spoon. Spread roughly over the pears, and cook for at least 40 minutes in the upper middle of the oven. The sponge should be golden brown and a skewer should come out cleanly. Serve immediately with the toffee sauce and lots of cream.

Pear and Chocolate Cake

This makes a great pudding with cream or custard, or is fantastic for tea. These cakes are very moist so put the tin on a baking tray to stop them oozing all over your oven. Variations, well worth trying, can be based on cherries and almonds, or apples and cinnamon – see below for quantities.

Serves 4 to 6
300g (10oz) pears (about 2), peeled, cored and cut into chunks – Conference are ideal
115g (4oz) unsalted butter
175g (6oz) self-raising flour
Pinch of salt
100g (4oz) milk chocolate chips
90g (3oz) caster sugar
2 medium eggs, beaten (we usually use 1½ large eggs, as we find it makes the mixture less gloopy)

Pre-heat the oven to 180°C/350°F/Gas 4. Grease a rectangular cake tin, 23x9cm (9x4in), with collapsible sides to get the cake out easily.

Put flour, salt and butter into a processor and pulse until it looks like fine breadcrumbs. Transfer to a bowl and add, in order, the sugar, 80g (3oz) of chocolate chips, and the pears. Stir in the eggs, then put the mixture into the tin. These cakes are very moist, so put the tin in a baking tray to stop them oozing everywhere. Bake for 50 minutes, the top should be crisp, but not too brown. When you take the cake out, put the rest of the chocolate chips on top so that they melt and stay in place. Leave to cool in the tin on a wire rack before turning out.

Omit pears and chocolate chips, and substitute:

75g (3oz) ground almonds

300g (10oz) sweet cherries, stoned and halved

¼ teaspoon almond essence

Handful almond slivers

Sprinkling of demerara sugar

Omit pears and chocolate chips, and substitute:

120g (4oz) toasted hazelnuts (see below)

300g (10½ oz) plums (about 8), stones removed and cut into small chunks. The plums can be firm but you may need to add more sugar to taste

Sprinkling of demerara sugar

Omit pears and chocolate chips, and substitute:

300g (10oz) dessert apples (2–3 apples), peeled, cored and cut into smallish chunks

½ teaspoon ground cinnamon

Grated zest of ½ a lemon

Sprinkling of demerara sugar

Cherry and Almond Version

Add the ground almonds to the cake mixture, at the same time as the caster sugar. Then add the cherries and almond essence. When the cake comes out of the oven, before dusting with demerara sugar, push the slivers of plain or toasted almond into the top of the cake – most easily done where the cherries meet the surface.

Plum and Hazelnut Version

Add the finely ground hazelnuts at the same time as the sugar, then add the plums. This version takes longer to cook, up to 1 hour, and then another 15 minutes with the top lightly covered with tinfoil to stop it browning too much. As soon as you remove the cake from the oven, press the whole nuts into the top of the cake, scatter the chopped nuts, and sprinkle with demerara sugar, which will melt slightly and hold the hazelnuts in place.

For the toasted hazelnuts

Preheat oven to 180°C/350°F/Gas 4. Spread the nuts on a baking tray and toast for approximately 5 minutes. Remove from the oven and, when cooled slightly, rub the nuts in your fingertips to remove any loose skin. Place 6 or so in a blender and pulse to form chunks for decoration on the top of the cake. Blitz the rest of the nuts in the blender until the resemble coarse sand.

Apple and Cinnamon Version

Add the cinnamon to the flour. Add the apples and lemon zest with the sugar. Dust with demerara sugar, as soon as the cake comes out of the oven to give it a crisp top.

Quinces

The Lost Fruit

Until the 19th-century, quinces were probably the most commonplace orchard fruit throughout Europe. Nowadays most people hardly know what a quince looks like – they have become the lost fruit.

Quinces, like so much of the orchard fruit we eat today, have their origins in Central Asia. The earliest known quinces grew wild in the foothills of the Caucasus Mountains between Persia and Turkmenistan, a seemingly inhospitable area that is actually very fertile and where many fruits thrived. The valleys below contained strategically important cities and channelled the paths of the old trade routes, along which quinces rapidly spread both eastwards and westwards.

By the 7th-century BC they had reached both Greece and China. Before the 3rd-century BC they were in Italy. They then spread throughout the Mediterranean. They had reached France by the time of Charlemagne and were cultivated in England during the 13th-century. By the beginning of the 19th-century, they had made their way into most areas of the world, including the Americas, which would support their cultivation. They occurred frequently in myth, custom, art and literature.

By the end of the 19th-century, sugar had become cheap and was freely available. This led to a change in taste, and the astringent flavour of the quince was no longer in demand. In the 20th-century, the labour-intensive preparation and cooking spelt its death.

Recently, interest has revived. A taste for sharper flavours based on Middle Eastern cooking has been boosted by our interest in other countries' culinary traditions. Quinces are also seen as exotic in a society that increasingly values something different from mass-produced food.

Unlike so many orchard fruits, quinces nowadays lack romantic names for the relatively few varieties in cultivation – although in China they were once known as the Golden Peaches of Samarkand, despite being so common that other fruits such as the pear and plum were much more highly valued.

Apart from their culinary value the other main reason to plant quinces is their visual appeal when covered in pinkish white blossom in spring and with golden fruit in autumn.

As quinces spread westwards from the Caucasus they rapidly reached the Middle East, and were carried on trading routes into the eastern Mediterranean by the commercial empires of the Greeks and Phoenicians, where they have played a significant part in the cultures of what are now Iran, Iraq and Syria. Biblical mythology talks of 'fruit' rather than naming the specific variety to be found in the Garden of Eden or described in the Song of Songs. However, they could have been quinces. Equally, one can simply argue that the whole point of God forcing Adam and Eve out of Eden was to prevent them eating the fruit of the Tree of Life and 'living forever' after consuming that of the Tree of Knowledge. By implication both trees were thus confined to a unique, symbolic, specimen within the equally symbolic garden.

The quince was probably the most widely available of the Mediterranean fruits from the classical period to the late Middle Ages. Quinces were specifically mentioned in Greek texts by the 6th-century BC and more generally referred to as Golden Apples. They can be hard to identify in some written sources of the period. The Greeks often used the word *melon* to refer to any round, hard fruit including apples and quinces, as well as the more specific nouns (*strythion* and *cydonia*) available to them for the fruit. The confusion between apples and quinces persisted into the Renaissance in the visual arts, with some artists painting or drawing quinces and others apples to illustrate well-known myths.

Below: These quinces may look blemished, but the fluffy grey down rubbing away shows they are ready to pick.

In Greece and the Eastern Mediterranean, quinces are still associated with weddings, fertility and sexual energy. It may be something to do with their curiously suggestive shapes and the sensuous down covering the ripening fruit. Whatever the reason, the association was formalised by the Athenian law-giver Solon in the 6th-century BC, who set down the role of quinces in wedding ceremonies, which have been passed down in the West through Plutarch's *Commentaries*, written in the late 1st-century. To this day, Greek wedding parties often eat a cake containing quinces baked with honey and sesame seeds to symbolise the couple's enduring commitment through good times and bad. They throw quinces at the bride and groom as they go to their new home, and present the bride with a quince to ensure fertility.

There are no records of quinces reaching Britain with the Romans, or indeed before the 13th-century, but it is not unlikely that some were grown during the Roman occupation. By the end of the Middle Ages, they had become well established and a dish of stuffed, baked quinces was amongst those served at Richard III's sumptuous Coronation Banquet in 1482.

Sometimes the association of quinces with fertility took on a medicinal meaning, as in the quince marmalades (oranges weren't used until the 1790s) of the early Tudor period. These contained almonds and were highly regarded by many including Queen Mary, desperate to conceive a son after her marriage to Philip of Spain in 1554. Unfortunately it didn't do it for her, nor did it work for the other Mary, Queen of Scots, who tried it as a seasickness remedy on the voyage from Calais to Scotland in 1561.

From the late Middle Ages until the 19th-century, quinces were commonly grown in Britain and used principally to make marmalade or jam and in the preparation of sweetmeats and puddings.

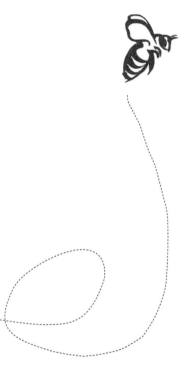

Right: The blossom of the quince tree is particularly pretty, making it a perfect tree for an ornamental garden.

QUINCES IN ART AND LITERATURE

Quinces occur from time to time in both art and literature, although far less frequently than, say, apples. In general, artists and writers needing to depict something concrete from the Bible have preferred the apple as the fruit of the Garden of Eden, which are often naturalistically depicted in Renaissance paintings of the Christ Child. They also fulfil the symbolic role of representing the Fall and Original Sin to be overcome by Christ's death. Interestingly, quinces are occasionally to be found substituting for apples in this manner in Venetian painting and have been so used in paintings of the Madonna and Child by both Bellini and Titian. Painters and re-tellers of classical mythology have likewise generally preferred to use golden apples to quinces, and they are relatively rare in both Greek painted pottery and sculpture and in the period from the Renaissance onwards.

There are, however, some significant exceptions. Bellini started, and Titian finished, a large and superb painting, now in the National Gallery of Art in Washington, USA, known as the *Feast of The Gods*. Although its classical sources are complicated, it shows a sort of heavenly picnic of sleepy gods and goddesses who have had rather too much to drink. Right in the centre is a nymph with one breast bared and holding a quince, shown at the moment when the lecherous Priapus was just about to jump on her. She was saved when his donkey brayed, waking the other picnickers. This quince has a clear symbolic role representing fertility, desirability and possibly an ironic contrast to the ideal state of ordered marriage.

Equally, there are examples of purely decorative quinces that are not intended to represent any more than the fruit itself and quite devoid of deeper meaning. For example, there is a very fine, very large and very realistic quince, now in the Ashmolean Museum in Oxford, Britain, modelled in glazed tinware pottery by the Della Robbia family.

Above: *The Feast of the Gods*, begun by Bellini and finished by Titian. An interesting, and rather unusual, example of quinces in painting. Probably an ironic comment on the sanctity of marriage.

Quinces appear in literature from time to time. Shakespeare, knowing his Plutarch, causes Juliet's old nurse, when anticipating her marriage, to say: '*We shall have dates and quinces in pastry*'. Edward Lear was well grounded in Greek myth and history and knew what he was doing when he wrote of the Owl and the Pussy-Cat getting...

> *...married next day,*
> *by the Turkey who lives on the hill.*
> *They dined on mince, and slices of quince,*
> *Which they ate with a runcible spoon.*

Quinces are briefly mentioned in the *Arabian Nights* and Chaucer's translation of *Romance of the Rose*, and are the subject of a poem entitled *The Quince* from 10th-century Spain. The Hispano-Arab poet Shafer ben Utman al-Mushafi, vizier to the Moorish ruler of Corboda Al Hakam the Second, draws an accurate and sensuous picture of the fruit itself, combined with his image of his lover's body and his lust to experience it.

It is yellow in colour, as if it wore a daffodil
tunic, and it smells like musk, a penetrating smell.

It has the perfume of a loved woman and the same
hardness of heart, but it has the colour of the
impassioned and scrawny lover.

Its pallor is borrowed from my pallor; its smell
is my sweetheart's breath.

When it stood fragrant on the bough and the leaves
had woven for it a covering of brocade,

I gently put up my hand to pluck it and to set it
like a censer in the middle of my room.

It had a cloak of ash-coloured down hovering over
its smooth golden body,

And when it lay naked in my hand, with nothing more than
its daffodil-coloured shift,

It made me think of her I cannot mention, and I feared
the ardour of my breath would shrivel it in my fingers.

Translated by A.L. Lloyd
(from Geoffrey Grigson's
Aphrodite quoted in Fruit
by Jane Grigson).

Looking back on it, it seems like a golden age with the orchards full of softly coloured hanging fruit at harvest time. It probably wasn't, but as a child you tend to believe things will never change.

CHRIS

QUINCES FOR HEALTH AND BEAUTY

Before modern drugs and cosmetics industries evolved, natural remedies played a far greater part in peoples' lives. Many claims were made for quinces – some correct, some downright dodgy. Since they are, for example, genuinely rich in vitamin C, flavonoids, antioxidants and pectin, they do help digestion. The vitamin content would boost immunity from disease in general and, significantly, the few sailors to return alive from Magellan's voyage around the world of 1522, although sick and exhausted, had probably been protected from the effects of scurvy by the quinces they ate on board. However, quinces, oranges and pomegranates were all believed to offer protection against everything from hair loss to plagues (the Black Death in particular – quince down was applied to plague sores ... without effect). Sir Thomas Elyot in his *Castel of Helth* of 1541 suggested cooked quinces '*preserveth the head from drunkeness*'. No dose was suggested – perhaps it was dependent on the likely intake!

Quinces have also been used in beauty products and, to this day, quince-based skin cream is used by many women who swear by its effects. Soaking the seeds (preferably from the cooked fruit) in water for a couple of weeks produces a pectin-based anti-inflammatory soothing gel. Nicholas Culpeper claimed it would soothe the sore breasts of women – no trivial matter in an age where everything associated with childbirth and infant care was fraught with danger, difficulty and infection. In France, the gel was used to make hair glossy. While the claims may be exaggerated they are by no means ridiculous, and the suggested remedies are likely to do more good and much less harm than many commercial products stuffed with legal but still dubious chemicals with yet unknown properties.

Quince Recipes

Lamb and Chickpea Tagine with Couscous

Serves 4

1kg (2lb) lamb shoulder (trimmed and cubed) or 4 lamb shanks

½ teaspoon cumin seeds

½ teaspoon coriander seeds

75g (3oz) butter

1 teaspoon ground ginger

½ teaspoon cayenne pepper

3 garlic cloves, crushed

2 onions, roughly chopped

250g (9oz) dried chickpeas, soaked overnight and rinsed

½ cinnamon stick

½ teaspoon ground cinnamon

4 tablespoons honey

1 large handful fresh coriander, roughly chopped

1 large quince, peeled but left whole

2 strips lemon rind, cut lengthwise

½ teaspoon saffron threads, dissolved in a little water

couscous (as desired, enough to serve 4)

People worry about cooking quinces, thinking there must be a lot of work involved since the flesh cannot be eaten raw. Very high-quality flesh can be extracted from roasted quinces with a minimum of effort, but this is not always appreciated by people who are already anxious about cooking with them. Quinces not only make excellent jelly but also ice-creams, puddings and sweets, as well as being a good partner to meats, especially lamb and game. This is a lovely Middle Eastern stew, combining sweet and spicy flavours. The chickpeas give body to the stew and the couscous soaks up the juices beautifully. You can alter the combinations and amounts of spices to suit your tastebuds!

Preheat the oven to 150°C/300°F/Gas 2. Grind the cumin and coriander seeds. Melt the butter in a casserole dish. Add the cumin, coriander, ginger and cayenne. Then add the garlic and onion. Coat with the butter. Add the lamb, stir and mix everything well.

Add 400ml (14fl oz) water, chickpeas, cinnamon stick, ground cinnamon, half the honey and a third of the coriander leaves. Bring to the boil, cover, put in the oven and cook for 1½ hours, or until the lamb is tender.

Put the quince in a saucepan just covered with water. Add the remaining honey and the lemon rind and bring to the boil, before simmering and poaching until tender (half an hour or so depending on the quince's size). Save the poaching liquid.

When the lamb is cooked, remove it and the chickpeas and keep them warm. Add about three tablespoons of the poaching liquid and the saffron to the meat juices. Reduce, taste and adjust the seasoning, if necessary.

Return the meat and the chickpeas to the pan, and add the quince. Cook the couscous according to the packet instructions, using half water and half quince poaching liquid. Fluff up the couscous with a fork, adding a splash of olive oil and salt (to taste) and pepper to taste. Serve the lamb on a bed of couscous and scatter the remaining coriander leaves on top.

Makes 1 to 2 small bottles

350ml (12fl oz) quince juice
  (about 2 large, ripe quinces)

50g (2oz) caster sugar

Pinch cinnamon

1 clove

1 white or black peppercorn

350ml (12fl oz) brandy

50g (2oz) almonds, blanched and
  skinned (optional)

Ratafia

Look in almost any reference book and you will find a different definition of ratafia: a spirit infused with almonds or fruit used to toast a deal or bargain, a 19th-century English biscuit or a French aperitif made from grape juice and brandy. It even appears in Georgette Heyer novels, where it is a drink frequently enjoyed by the ladies, but scorned by the gentlemen of the time.

Its origins are obscure, although the most attractive is that it was the liqueur drunk at the ceremonies ratifying European treaties from the 15th-century onwards. The name could come from the Latin rata fiat *(let the deal be settled). The recipe below is based on one in* The Modern Cook, *written by Vincent la Chapelle in 1733.*

Cut up and juice the quinces, using an electric juicer. Put the juice in a pan, bring to the boil and then remove from the heat and cool. Put the sugar, cinnamon, clove and peppercorn into a pan with 50ml (2fl oz) water and heat gently until the sugar has dissolved. Remove from the heat and cool. Pour the juice, brandy and sugar solution into a bowl and stir so that the three combine. Add the almonds, if using. Pour into a jar, seal and leave in a cool, dark place for 2–3 months.

Strain the liquid through a muslin cloth. Do not squeeze the cloth as you want the liqueur to be as clear as possible. Finally, decant into a bottle and seal, or as Vincent la Chapelle charmingly puts it 'bottles flopped very close.' It will keep almost indefinitely.

Makes between 12 and 20, depending
on finished discs

250g (9oz) quinces, peeled and
halved

210g (7½ oz) caster sugar

Juice ¼ lemon

50g (2oz) small pieces of crystallised
fruit, preferably red.

50g (2oz) blanched almonds,
chopped

100g (3½ oz) good-quality dark
chocolate

Tudor Aphrodisiacs

*The paste at the centre of these chocolates was
originally known as Quince Marmalade, or Dry
Suckets of Quince, and would have been eaten at
the end of a banquet. The chocolates were sometimes
wrapped in gold foil and were considered to be
aphrodisiacs.*

Put the quince in a saucepan, cover with water
and bring to the boil. Cover the pan and simmer
until the quinces are soft, for about half an hour.
Drain, setting the quinces aside and reserving the
cooking liquid. Core the quinces while warm and
mash, or purée the fruit in a food processor.

Measure 55ml (2fl oz) of the cooking liquid
into a saucepan. Add the sugar, dissolve over a low
heat, stirring until the syrup is clear, and then boil
without stirring until it is thick and caramelly.
The mixture is ready when a little dropped into
cold water forms a ball. Add the purée and continue
boiling and stirring until very thick and pulling
away from the sides.

Remove from the heat, add the lemon juice, fruit
and nuts, and mix well. Turn onto a smooth surface,
lined with clingfilm. As soon as it is cool enough,
roll the mixture into a sausage shape, using the
clingfilm to wrap it.

Refrigerate overnight. Cut the sausage into
chunks the size of after-dinner chocolates; put
them into a container lined with greaseproof paper
and form them into rough discs with your fingers,
ignoring the squishiness! Melt the chocolate in
a bowl set over hot water, stirring occasionally.
Remove the bowl from the heat. Dip the pieces in
the chocolate so they are completely coated, using
two forks or cocktail sticks. Refrigerate the now
completed chocolates. Once hard, you can wrap
the sweetmeats in gold foil to transform them into
beautifully tasty aphrodisiacs!

Plums

A Treat for the Senses

If you possibly can, you should have at least one plum tree, for the blossom is beautiful and the fruit at its best is memorably delicious. Much of the visual charm of plums lies in the range of their skin colour, the overlying blooms of whitish grey, and the semi-translucent, or even almost transparent, juicy flesh within. These skin colours range from intense reds, purples and oranges to greens and yellows. At the point of ripeness they can be truly jewel-like. Plums make superb jam. No summer would be really complete without eating some home-grown plums, gushingly sweet, and allowing juice to run down one's chin like a child!

TYPES OF PLUMS

Unlike apples, which slide about within artificial classifications of cookers, eaters and cider apples, plums can fairly easily be divided into separate categories. In some cases these are sufficiently distinctive to correspond to different species within the general *Prunus* family to which all plums belong.

These categories include the sloe (*P. spinosa*), the cherry plum (*P. cerasifera*), and the wild plum or bullace (*P. institita*), from which the French Mirabelle is derived and which may have been a precursor of the damson. Normal domestic plums are generally known botanically as *P. domestica* and they appear to result from hybridisation between the cherry plum and the bullace. The Japanese plums tend to be derived from the species *P. triflora,* although they are sadly unsuitable for growing in this country.

The sloe is a hedgerow tree with vicious spines and a small bitter fruit – it does, however, provide an excellent flavouring for gin! The bullace, little grown now and found in hedgerows,

tends to produce a sharp-flavoured fruit that is only mellowed by leaving it on the tree well into autumn. Most plums, whether cookers or eaters, tend to have reddish or purple skins and a juicy fruit surrounding the stone. Damsons, whose relatively acidic fruit is excellent in gins, jams and cooking, tend to be smaller and oval in shape, with a dark purple-blue skin. It is believed their name is a corruption of Damascus and indicates their origins in the Near East.

Three other distinct categories of plum exist. The Myrobalan or cherry plum (*P. cerasifera*) is principally decorative, with small round red or yellow fruits. Gages are yellow or green, luscious and sweet, sometimes with an almost transparent flesh. The lovely sweet golden yellow Mirabelles of France are not much found in this country, but anyone who has eaten a tarte aux Mirabelles or drunk the eau de vie produced from them will know what we are missing. Genes that control the production of pigments (known as anthocyanins and cyanins) are actually responsible for the fine variations of colour we see in many of the best plums as they ripen through the summer. Plum blossom, although vulnerable to frost, also makes a valuable addition to any garden.

HISTORY

It seems a fair assumption that wild and cultivated plums have been common throughout Europe since classical times. Homer mentioned plums in his descriptions of orchards. Roman literary references do not seem to predate the first-century AD although Pliny describes twelve varieties including the damson, by then long-established in Italy. He expressed surprise that plums had not been mentioned by Cato, writing some 250 years before him. One way or another we have certainly had plums in Britain for a very long time. Wild plums, sloes, and the rather similar bullaces, have occurred naturally in Britain since the Ice Age. Plum stones have been found in archaeological sites as ancient as the late Iron Age, and many stones from cultivated varieties date from the Roman period.

It is likely that plums were cultivated in Roman Britain, survived at least in the monasteries through the Dark Ages and were generally present in medieval times, although less frequently mentioned than apples or pears.

The great fruit-growing depression of the 15th-century seems to have reduced stocks and cultivation to fairly minimal levels, but they were revived by continental imports during the reign of Henry VIII. Damsons appear to have been amongst the most popular varieties, as they are now, as recent archaeological proof has shown. When the hull of Henry VIII's flagship, the *Mary Rose*, which had sunk in the Solent in 1545, was raised up in 1982 it was found to contain several hundred plum stones of five recognisable varieties, including the damson. It was rumoured that the stones were even discovered to be viable – but, perhaps unsurprisingly, we have been quite unable to trace anyone who knows where the resulting trees might be now!

Continental imports continued to rejuvenate the national stock of plums throughout the 16th- and 17th-centuries. The gardening writers of the period frequently commented on this. In 1597, Gerard stated that the number of varieties had increased greatly during his time and he himself held some sixty of them in his garden. John Tradescant, the Cecil family's gardener at Hatfield House in Hertfordshire, had played a considerable part in the introduction of new varieties of all sorts of fruit, plums included, in the early 17th-century. His role was acknowledged by John Parkinson, writing in 1629 and mentioning sixty-one different varieties. By the second half of the century, Evelyn mentioned seventy-five types of plum and Worlidge some seventy. Some varieties known since the 17th-century are still in cultivation today (for example, Blue Pendrigon and Amber Primordian – now known as Catalonia).

The 18th-century saw little by way of real innovation, although considerable confusion arose when stock of the same

variety of plum was relabelled, often by nurserymen hopeful
of higher sales. Langley and Swift, writing in the 1730s, spoke
of '*at least twenty totally good varieties*' a number probably
similar to, and including most of the same types, as would
have been the case some 50 or 60 years before.

An apparent 18th-century discovery, the Greengage turns
out to be a fascinating case of misnaming. In 1629, Parkinson
mentioned a plum known as the Verdoch, which is probably
the present-day Greengage or Reine Claude. It seems to have
reached Italy by the 15th-century, where it was known as
the Verdochia, from Greece and Armenia, and subsequently
arrived in France during the reign of Francis 1, after whose
wife, Reine Claude, it was named. The name Greengage arose
when some specimens were sent from Paris to Sir Thomas
Gage at Hengrave Hall by his brother John. The attached label
was subsequently lost, causing the gardener to simply call
them Green Gages after his employer. By 1729, both names
were separately listed, and since 1739 the British one has
been in common usage.

One respectable plum, Coe's Golden Drop (a remarkably
descriptive name for what is still a moderately good fruit),
was discovered in 1779. By the time the (future) RHS founded
its botanical garden in Chiswick in the early 19th-century, it
thought it possessed 282 varieties of plum – sadly, few turned
out to be of any merit and many were identical to each other,
simply masquerading under different names. William Forsyth,
a founding member of the RHS, who claimed some twenty-
seven good varieties existed in 1805, was nearer the mark.

The 19th-century saw new discoveries of, and revived
interest in, plums. An impressive concentration on
horticultural technology and selective breeding was
somewhat confounded by the discovery of a chance seedling
in 1840. It turned out to be Victoria, probably the one plum
everyone can still name today. This, at first, cast into the

shade the work of two sets of very competent British fruit growers, the Rivers and Laxton families – as well as the extensive breeding programmes in the USA, especially at Princes Nursery in Long Island. However, they gave us plums we still consume today – Early Rivers, Czar, Laxton's Gage and Jefferson are just a few – and there's no doubt that the best plums date from the 19th-century, apart from the Greengage and Marjorie's Seedling, which was discovered by chance in 1912.

Despite all this work, plums remain something of an endangered species. A number of the old favourites such as Victoria and Marjorie's Seedling are widely grown but little has come on to take their place. If more people knew how good a perfect home-grown plum tastes, growers might try to develop a variety that combines frost- and disease-resistance with flavour and appearance.

PLUMS IN MYTHOLOGY, LITERATURE AND ART

There's no getting round it: plums play nothing like the role that apples do. They occur in literature, though, in earlier examples either as a casual image or a part of a list of fruits (in Chaucer's translation of the *Romance of the Rose,* for example). Keats chose the image of a ripening plum to contrast with excessive human ambition, in his famous sonnet on fame.

How fevered is the man who cannot look
Upon his mortal days with temperate blood,
Who vexes all the leaves of his life's book,
And robs his fair name of its maidenhood;
It is as if the rose should pluck herself,
Or the ripe plum finger its misty bloom,
As if a Naiad, like a meddling elf,
Should darken her pure grot with muddy gloom;
But the rose leaves herself upon the briar,
For winds to kiss and grateful bees to feed,
And the ripe plum still wears its dim attire;
The undisturbed lake has crystal space;
Why then should man, teasing the world for grace,
Spoil his salvation for a fierce miscreed?

More than a hundred years later, damsons occur in the
passionate poetry that resulted from the First World War.
By July of 1915, the poet Edward Thomas had enlisted in the
Artists Rifles, in which he survived until his death in 1917.
In November 1915, he wrote *There's Nothing Like the Sun*,
overcast with melancholy that is both generally autumnal
and also seems to reflect his sense of transience at still
being alive in a world being torn apart while the last damsons
miraculously persevere in late autumn:

November has begun
Yet never shone the sun as fair as now
While the sweet last-left damsons from the bough
With spangles of the morning's storm drop down
Because the starling shakes it, whistling what
Once swallows sang.

James Joyce introduces plums into what many critics have
called the first modern novel, *Ulysses*. This brilliant although

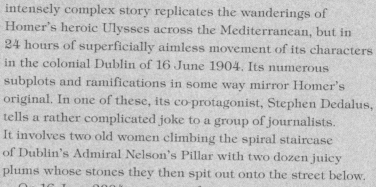

intensely complex story replicates the wanderings of Homer's heroic Ulysses across the Mediterranean, but in 24 hours of superficially aimless movement of its characters in the colonial Dublin of 16 June 1904. Its numerous subplots and ramifications in some way mirror Homer's original. In one of these, its co-protagonist, Stephen Dedalus, tells a rather complicated joke to a group of journalists. It involves two old women climbing the spiral staircase of Dublin's Admiral Nelson's Pillar with two dozen juicy plums whose stones they then spit out onto the street below.

On 16 June 2004 a street performance of a play based on this incident was enacted on the original site chosen in the novel. However, the Pillar, a symbol of British colonial occupation, was blown up by the IRA in 1966, and had been replaced with a new Millennium Tower.

Plums occur in a number of poems by William Carlos Williams, for example. Bertholt Brecht also wrote a rather enigmatic children's poem about a plum tree.

> *The plum tree in the yard's so small*
> *It's hardly like a tree at all...*

In the visual arts, plums occur slightly more often. They appear in many still-life paintings and botanical illustrations. There is a superb Chardin still life of a basket of plums, a glass of water and two cherries, where the artist captures the play of light on surface and achieves splendid harmonies of tone and colour. Braque painted some purple plums in a still life as one of his many explorations of space and reality, and there is a small oil by Samuel John Peploe of a pear and plums with a knife. Sometimes they represent some greater symbolic theme. The mutability of all living things in many Dutch *vanitas* paintings is heightened by the transient bloom of ripe plums that will soon decay. Often they are simply an

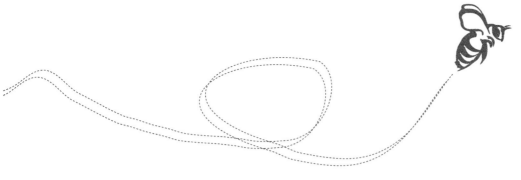

Left: Victoria plums come in a wide range of colours.
Overleaf: The pale pink blossom of sloe trees is beautiful. The fruits are too tart to eat, but can be used to make delicious flavoured gin (see page 205).

illustration of a plum as plum, as in many illustrated pomonas and other books on fruit growing. In the East, though, it is a different matter: plum blossom is a central subject of much Chinese art, and has symbolic significance.

PLUM BRANDIES, SLIVOVITZ AND MIRABELLE EAU DE VIE
Plums can be used as a base or flavouring for a variety of spirits and brandies. Distilled to make plum brandy, they produce sometimes rather fiery liquors called Slivovice in the Czech lands and Slivovitz in the Balkans. The plum is the national fruit of Serbia and Slivovitz the national drink. Locals, who consume it enthusiastically, claim that it does not produce hangovers and may even cure them: those who have drunk it in Western Europe might be forgiven certain scepticism. In France, a much more delicate and less fearsome eau de vie is Mirabelle, distilled from the eponymous little plums. This is, even now, typically an artisan rather than an industrial operation and utilises copper stills of considerable antiquity.

PLUMS FOR EATING AND COOKING
Although many imported eating plums can be something of a disappointment (a wonderfully uniform appearance disguises a bland flavour and woolly texture), the best home-grown plums are a delight worth the risks of growing them. In a good year, the visual delight of a red or deep purple skin flecked with oranges and yellows is followed by succulent flesh with a fine balance of acid and sweetness. For cooking, a little more acid is helpful, and damsons in particular have huge potential in tarts, jellies, jams, gins and ice-creams. The amount of sugar you need to add for puddings such as pies and crumbles is clearly dependent on the underlying level of acidity.

When the fruit ripened, we had huge gluts of plums and apples. We got tummy ache from eating them, and the kitchen always seemed full of pans making plum jam on the Aga.

CHRIS

Plum Recipes

Plum Sauce

450g (1lb) plums or, ideally,
   damsons
Sugar as required (up to 120g/4oz
   for damsons; very little for ripe
   Victorias)
Juice of half a lemon
Star anise, cinnamon stick
A piece of peeled fresh ginger,
   grated finely.

*The Roman cookery writer Apicius gave a recipe for
fish in plum sauce. We tried to make it; for modern
tastes the result was excessively sharp and very highly
spiced, although it would no doubt have covered up
any deterioration in the fish due to a hot climate.
The recipe below can be used with most fatty meats
and you could also use it with an oily fish such as
mackerel or herring.*

Halve and stone the plums, cooking them gently with
the sugar (if needed), the spices and the lemon juice
for long enough until they are reduced to a purée
(perhaps 20 minutes). Only add water to stop them
from sticking. Sieve (it is essential not to liquidise
the woody cinnamon and star anise), and then
liquidise the resulting mixture. Return to the heat
and adjust the seasoning, serving warm. Some
recipes include cloves, chillies and other herbs –
once you are familiar with the basic method you
can adjust it as you see fit.

Damson Jam

450g (1lb) damsons, halved and
   stoned
450g (1lb) jam or granulated sugar
   (jam sugar is quicker)

*This glorious clear colour is so intense that you may
feel it is as much a table decoration as a culinary treat.
General information on jam-making can be found on
page 195.*

Simmer the fruits in 140ml (5fl oz) water until soft.
Add the sugar and simmer gently, stirring until it
has completely dissolved. Turn the heat up and boil
the jam until it reaches setting point. When the jam
is set, add a small knob of butter to remove the scum

or spoon it off with a metal spoon. Leave for 10 minutes to settle and then pour into sterilised jars and seal. Makes just over 2 jars and works just as well for plums or greengages.

Damson Ice-cream

This may not be one of the more usual ice-creams, but it is certainly one of the most delicious. Try to remove from the freezer 15 minutes before you would like to eat it.

450g (1lb) whole damsons
120g (4oz) soft, light brown sugar
4 egg yolks
120g (4oz) icing sugar
280ml (½ pint) double cream
2 tablespoons iced water

Put the damsons into a saucepan with the brown sugar and 280ml (½ pint) water, and bring to the boil. Cover and simmer the fruit until it is tender – about 10 minutes depending on the ripeness of the damsons. Press the stewed fruit through a sieve. Discard the stones and chill the purée in the refrigerator.

In a bowl, set over a saucepan of simmering water, beat the egg yolks with the icing sugar until the mixture is warm but not hot. Take the bowl off the heat and continue beating until the mixture has tripled its original volume, then chill it in the refrigerator.

Whisk the cream with the iced water until it holds soft peaks. Combine the damson purée, egg mixture and whipped cream and whisk them lightly together. Freeze in an ice-cream maker following the manufacturer's instructions. Or place in the freezer, removing and vigorously whisking the partially frozen ice several times.

See also, Plum and Hazelnut Cake, page 129. Or, Damson Gin and Sloe Gin, page 205.

Cherries

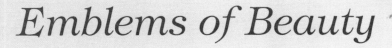

Emblems of Beauty

Loveliest of trees, the cherry now
Is hung with bloom along the bough,
And stands about the woodland ride
Wearing white for Eastertide.

This poem, taken from A. E. Housman's *A Shropshire Lad* sums up many peoples' vision of a cherry tree: pure beauty. What an amazing tree that gives us such a visual feast combined with the most delicious fruit.

TYPES OF CHERRY

The word cherry comes directly from the old French *cherise* and the Latin *cerasus*, which, in turn came from *karsu*, an Accadian word used by the Assyrians and Babylonians who first cultivated them. Although it is to the Middle East that we look for the origins of cultivated cherries, wild cherry trees have grown in Western Europe since prehistoric times. By today's standards, the fruits were small and unpalatable, but many people ate them.

Prunus avium is the wild European cherry, which grows all over Western and Central Europe and is probably the ancestor of our present sweet cherry. The trees grow up to 18m (60ft) and their name comes from the fact that birds love their fruits. These are small and dark, but sweet, and are called geans or mazzards today. They are known to have been eaten by the prehistoric Lake Dwellers of Switzerland.

Prunus cerasus is a much smaller tree or bush with sourer fruit. Cultivated sour cherries divide into Morellos and Amarelles. Morellos have dark fruits and possibly came to Western Europe via Southern Spain – the name Morello means Little Moor. Amarelles are also known as Red Morellos and are paler. These are called *griottes* in France, where they are widely used in confectionery and to flavour eau de vie. Dukes (or Royales in France) are a hybrid of the two. They probably originated in the Medoc region of France, the name being mis-translated into May Duke and later shortened to Duke.

Japanese or flowering cherries were developed in the Far East as purely ornamental trees. Their blossom and autumn colours are often spectacular but they rarely bear fruit.

CULTIVATED CHERRIES

Cherries were known to be cultivated in Mesopotamia by the Assyrian King Sargon II in the 8th-century BC. He was probably not the first to cultivate them but he increased their popularity because he apparently liked their fragrance.

In the 5th-century BC, Herodotus described a race of Scythians called Argippaeans from the northern shores of the Black Sea. They lived almost exclusively on a type of cherry called Ponticum. Each family lived at the base of a tree, which was covered with lengths of white felt in winter, presumably to protect the inhabitants as well as the blossom. The cherries were strained to make a thick juice called aschy. *'They lap this up with their tongues, and also mix it with milk for a drink'*, with the left-over sediment being made into cakes and eaten later instead of meat.

According to Pliny, it is the Roman general and gourmet, Lucullus, who deserves the credit for bringing cultivated cherries to Italy in 74 BC. He had gone to fight Mithridates VI and returned victorious, bringing vast wealth and cherries. Since the war was fought in Pontus, on the shores of the Black Sea, these are probably the same fruits mentioned by Herodotus. One of the towns fought over was Cerasus (now Giresun in Turkey). This is sometimes credited as the origin

of the name *Cerasus,* but it is more likely that the town was a trade centre and was named after the fruit which was so important to the local economy. Cherries reached Britain fairly soon after arriving in Italy, and immediately became popular. Right through the Middle Ages, their brief season was enjoyed by everyone; in *Piers Plowman*, William Langland describes the poor people mostly living on vegetables but also enjoying baked apples and cherries. Fruit was often given as a gift, and in Spenser's *Faerie Queen*, Diana's maid is allured with:

Pleasing gifts for her purvey'd
Queen apples and red cherries from the tree.

Little was done to improve varieties, though, until the reign of Henry VIII. Soon after he came to the throne in 1509, he began a campaign to make Britain self-sufficient in fruit, and became especially fond of cherries. His fruiterer, Richard Harris, planted vast orchards at the New Garden at Teynham in Kent, which was the equivalent of today's national collection at nearby Brogdale. Mainland Europe had taken a greater interest in cultivating cherries and had many more varieties. In France, cherries were especially popular, and in 1364 King Charles V planted 115 apples, 100 pears, 150 plums and 1,125 cherries at the royal gardens at Tournelles and St-Paul. Many of these European varieties were brought over and planted in the rapidly spreading orchards of Kent.

The predominance of cherry orchards in Kent is not accidental; Kent was the perfect place to establish cherry orchards. It was near the markets of London and had the well-drained sandy soil that the trees liked. It was also not a county of great landowners, and the divisive method of strip cultivation had never been established. Most farmers actually owned the land they worked, and this was a great incentive for long-term projects such as orchards. In medieval times, an orchard solely

Left: *Landscape with Figures Gathering Cherries* by François Boucher, 1768.

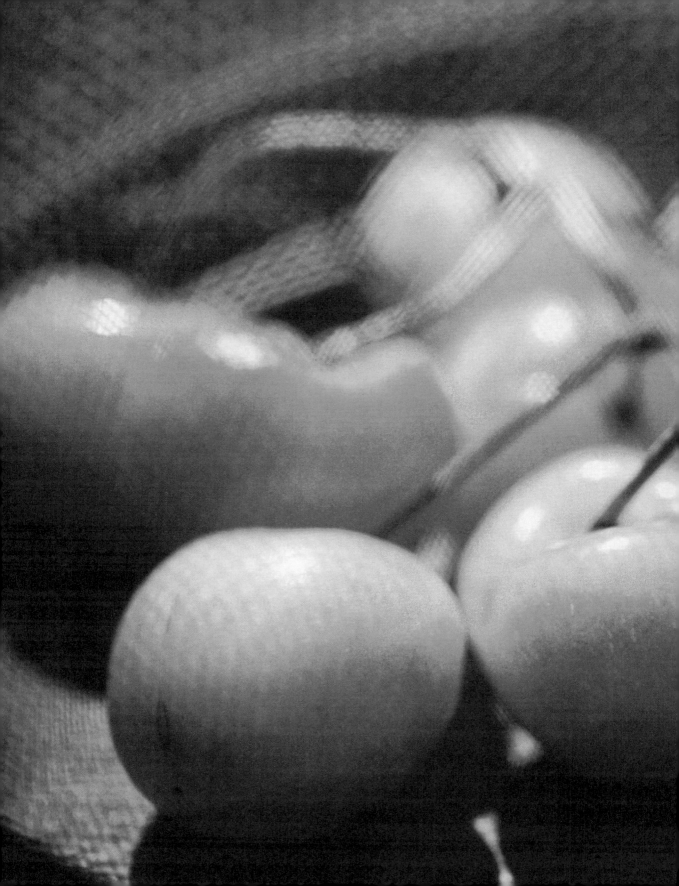

devoted to cherries had been called a *cherruzerd* or *orto cersor,* and these were now planted throughout the county. John Tradescant continued Richard Harris' work in the 17th-century, and cherry orchards grew up all along the banks of the Thames.

Cherry orchards flourished during the 18th- and 19th-centuries, but in the 20th-century the huge size of the trees made picking the fruit a problem. As Christopher Stocks describes in his book *Forgotten Fruits* trees were often over 15m (50ft) tall and harvesting required specialised equipment and manpower. The cumbersome wooden ladders often damaged the fruit, as well as the following year's buds which grow just beside the current year's stalks. Smaller trees had been developed for other fruits, and many cherry orchards were dug up and either replanted with fruits such as apples, or abandoned. Towards the end of the 20th-century this changed with the introduction of dwarfing rootstocks such as Colt and Gisela. Cherries could now be harvested as easily as other fruits and gradually they were replanted.

Above: Fruit blossom has huge
cultural significance in the Far East.
Thought the trees may not produce
edible fruit, their flowering signifies
a rite of spring.

This recovery has also been helped by the establishment of
Cherry Aid in 2008. This is a campaign that unites all cherry
lovers – from growers to chefs to producers of drinks and
members of the general public. It aims to get everyone eating
and growing British cherries, and is a major force in saving
our existing orchards. Every year, Cherry Day is celebrated on
a Saturday in mid-July (see Events on page 268 for details).

CHERRIES IN ART AND LITERATURE
In Christian art and writings, cherries have a somewhat
ambiguous place. Their red colour means they are often used
to represent the blood of Christ; their sweetness means they
are also associated with pleasure and paradise, and an antidote
to the cause of original sin, the apple. Many paintings such
as Memling's *Mother and Child with Two Angels* in the Uffizi
Gallery in Florence show Christ with both apples and cherries
to symbolise these two aspects of Christianity. The *Gospel
of Pseudo-Matthew* was written in the 8th-century, and forms

part of the New Testament apocrypha of writings, which
aimed to describe Jesus' childhood. The Flight into Egypt
is described in some detail and, apparently, a palm tree bore
cherries instead of dates to refresh Mary, Joseph and Jesus on
their long journey. This in turn inspired *The Cherry-Tree Carol*.
Here, the events take place on the way to Bethlehem while
Mary is still pregnant. They stop in a cherry orchard and Mary
asks Joseph to pick some fruit for her. He angrily replies that
the father of her child should pick the fruit, at which point
Jesus apparently speaks out from the womb and commands
the tree to lower its branches so Mary can reach the cherries.

Their short season and sweetness means cherries are used
throughout literature to symbolise beauty and the brief joys
of earthly life. 'Fresh, rosy cherries' innocently enhance
the garden in Guillaume de Lorris' part of the *Romance of
the Rose* in the 13th-century, but gradually they move towards
earthly passion, with William Shakespeare using the seductive
idea of cherry lips in many of his plays, and Thomas
Campion's poem *There is a Garden in her Face* continuing
the theme around 1617.

There is a Garden in her face,
Where Roses and white Lilies grow;
A heav'nly paradice is that place,
Wherein all pleasant fruits do flow.
There Cherries grow, which none may buy
Till Cherry ripe themselves doe cry.

Those Cherries fayrely doe enclose
Of Orient Pearle a double row;
Which when her lovely laughter shows,
They look like Rose-buds fill'd with snow.
Yet them nor Peere nor Prince can buy,
Till Cherry ripe themselves doe cry.

Her Eyes like Angels watch them still;
Her Browes like bended bowes doe stand,
Threatening with piercing frownes to kill
All that attempt with eye or hand
Those sacred Cherries to come nigh,
Till Cherry ripe themselves doe cry.

More poignant is Chekhov's play *The Cherry Orchard*, where an entire family base their life around an old and uneconomic orchard. A whole way of life seems to be crumbling when Mrs Ranevsky says: *'Oh, my orchard! – my dear, my sweet, my beautiful orchard! My life, my youth, my happiness, goodbye! goodbye!'*

CHERRY FESTIVALS AND FOLKLORE

Unlike fruits such as pears, cherries have always been enjoyed by people from all walks of life and, historically, their brief season was seen as a good excuse for a party. Medieval cherry fairs took place in the orchards; the fruit was picked and sold and afterwards there was drinking, dancing and general merrymaking. These have largely died out now, but, in Japan similar (if less bawdy) festivals are held to celebrate the cherry blossom in spring. Competitions and games were part of medieval festivals and according to the Venetian ambassador at the time of James I, one woman ate 20lb (9kg) of cherries at a festival in Kent. Cherry spitting was also popular, and even today National Cherry Spitting competitions survive in Switzerland and New Zealand. The game of cherry pit, described in Shakespeare's *Twelfth Night*, involves a play on the meanings of throwing (or spitting) cherry stones into a small pit or hole.

Fruit blossom has huge cultural significance in the Far East. Though the trees may not produce edible fruit, their flowering signifies a rite of spring.

Double cherries were worn as earrings, often to encourage lovers to eat them off the wearer as described in D. H. Lawrence's *Cherry Robbers*:

Against the haystack a girl stands laughing at me,
Cherries hung round her ears,
Offers me her scarlet fruit.

This is another tradition that is threatened by the 21st-century: some supermarkets specify that each fruit must be on a single stem!

The superstitions around this fruit are many. Some cherries are regarded as witch's tree in the north-east of Scotland, whereas in Wester Ross a stick of the same wood is prized as it is said to prevent the walker from getting lost. A good harvest was guaranteed if the first fruit was picked by a woman who had given birth to her first child; while in other areas, cherry blossom could not be used to decorate the church for a wedding.

MEDICINAL AND OTHER USES

Quite apart from the beauty of the blossom and the taste of the fruit, cherry trees also have other uses. The wood is hard and attractive and ideal for furniture making and turning, as well as firewood. Green dye can be extracted from the leaves and fruits and, in times gone by, the gum (sap) was thought to be beneficial. Culpeper states in his *Herbal* of 1826: '*The gum of the cherry-tree dissolved in wine is good for a cold, cough, and hoarseness of the throat; mendeth the colour in the face, sharpeneth the eye-sight, provoketh appetite, and helpeth to break and expel the stone.*' Was there anything it didn't cure?

Mrs Grieve's *Modern Herbal* of 1931 recommended that the stalks be used in the form of an infusion or decoction with ½oz (15g) stalks to a pint of water. As with the gum, this seemed to be a cure for almost anything. The stones are poisonous in large quantities but small doses stimulate respiration and improve digestion.

The cherries themselves contain a high level of antioxidants, which are thought to reduce the risk of heart disease and some cancers. They may also help with the pain of arthritis and gout, but, back in the Middle Ages, all fruit was regarded with a certain amount of suspicion. In the 13th-century, Scottish mathematician, magician and astrologer, Michael Scott, described them as *'In every way pernicious'* in his *Mensa Philosophica*, which has been variously translated as *The Philosopher's Banquet* or *The Science of Dining*. He was undoubtedly a learned, if eccentric, man and it is surprising that he took so violently against them at a time when most people regarded them as helpful against the Black Death. Later Culpeper wrote that sweet cherries contained little nourishment but that tart or sour fruits could be used to treat the few ailments that the gum couldn't cure.

CHERRY DRINKS
Kirsch, or eau de vie de Kirsch, as it is known in France, is a white brandy distilled from black cherries, with the stones left whole. Maraschino is a gentler drink made from Marasca cherries which grow along the Dalmatian coast and in Italy. The stones are crushed and the kernels give the drink its almond flavour. It is sweeter and fruitier than kirsch, often with added honey. For cherry brandy, the fruits are soaked in brandy and the drink is then sweetened with sugar and sometimes flavoured with kirsch. A splendid cocktail based on this is the Percy Special which is half cherry brandy and half whisky. Supposedly created by the 10th Duke of Northumberland, it is traditionally drunk before hunt meets and may account for some erratic riding!

CHERRIES IN THE KITCHEN

Glace cherries tend to adorn the tops of supermarket cakes and can be tasteless unless you get ones that have been well candied. The gardener and cook, Christopher Lloyd, remembers being sent Madeira cakes at school containing exactly 122 glace cherries for a now-forgotten reason. He loved the cakes:

However, Jane Grigson is, I'm sure rightly, so disdainful of these tasteless cherries that I have switched to almonds.

Maraschino cherries are, similarly, often poor imitations of what they should be, with too much synthetic flavouring. They should be stoned, bleached, coloured red or green and soaked in syrup and almond oil – avoid any you see with too many E numbers!

Cherries mix well with lemon, orange, cinnamon, mace, vanilla, nutmeg and almonds, and complement brandy, chocolate and all game. Cherry liqueurs are popular world-wide, and in France griottes are used almost exclusively surrounded by kirsch and encased in chocolate. Sour cherries are especially popular in savoury meat dishes in central Europe, and black cherries have immortalised themselves in Black Forest Gateau, for which we give a recipe on the following pages.

Cherry Recipes

Cherry Sauce

This sauce is traditionally served with duck, but also complements ham or turkey. It is equally good with hot or cold meat. It is best with fresh cherries when they are in season but tinned are a fine substitute.

3 oranges
1 lemon
1 tablespoon redcurrant jelly
150ml (¼ pint) port or red wine
   or Madeira
2 tablespoons stock or roasting
   juices
Thyme, rosemary or a couple
   of bay leaves, if you wish.
Pepper
175g (6oz) black cherries, pitted

Take the zest of the lemon and one orange and simmer in a little water so the zest is covered, until soft. Then drain.

Put the juice from the oranges and the lemon into a pan with the zest. Add the jelly, wine, stock and herbs. Whisk until everything is mixed and then boil until reduced by half.

Add pepper to taste, then the cherries, and simmer until cooked. Pour over and around the meat and serve the rest in a jug.

Clafoutis

Bake this in an attractive dish that you can put on the table, as it is quite messy to serve!

Serves 4-6
50g (2oz) unsalted butter
4 eggs
125g (4oz) caster sugar
50g (2oz) plain flour
250ml (7fl oz) milk
1 teaspoon vanilla extract
450g (1lb) sweet cherries, destalked
   and pitted if you wish. Tinned
   cherries are okay but need
   to be drained very well
Icing sugar

Pre-heat the oven to 190°C/375°F/Gas 5. Melt the butter. Whisk the eggs in a big bowl using an electric hand-mixer: as this will give you a better batter than in a processor. Add the sugar, then the flour, then the melted butter, and, finally, the milk and vanilla extract, whisking each one in well.

Lightly butter a 23cm (9in) dish. The base needs to be completely flat and the batter will cook more evenly if the sides are straight. Spread the cherries over the base of the dish and pour in the batter. Bake for about 40 minutes until golden brown and just setting. Sprinkle with icing sugar and serve warm.

Black Forest Gateau

*This is a seriously rich, indulgent cake, originally
trendy in the 1970s but now, justifiably, enjoying
a revival. There are two versions, one for when you
can get fresh cherries and one for the rest of the year
so you can enjoy it at any time.*

Preheat the oven to 170˚C/325˚F/Gas 3. Grease two
20cm (7½in) cake tins with removable bases.
Line the bases with greaseproof paper. (If using
a single 23cm/9in tin, cook for 50–60 minutes at
180˚C/350˚F/Gas 4 and cut into three layers. This
version will need a bit more filling and chocolate.)

Sift the flour, baking powder and cocoa into a
large bowl. Add the butter, sugar and eggs.

Mix roughly with a fork so the flour doesn't fly
everywhere, and then mix with an electric hand-
whisk, moving the whisk so you get as much air
as possible into the mixture. You can mix it in a
processor but the cake may not rise well as you
won't get as much air into the mixture.

Add 1 or 2 tablespoons of warm water so the
mixture plops off a spoon. Divide between the two
tins and bake in the middle of the oven for about
40 minutes until a skewer comes cleanly out of
the centre.

Leave to cool for a minute or two, then run a
knife round the edge and turn the cakes out onto
a wire rack, removing the paper from the base.

Put the cherries, sugar and kirsch into a small
saucepan and simmer until the cherries are soft.
Leave to cool. Or mix the conserve with the kirsch.
Whip the cream so it forms soft peaks.

Grate the chocolate using a peeler, so you get
bigger shavings. Level the top of one cake and then
cut each cake in half horizontally. Spread fruit and
cream on each layer and pile them up. Spread a
layer of cream on the top and sprinkle with the
chocolate. If you are feeling very glamorous you
can add cherries dipped in chocolate to the top!

Serves 6

225g (8oz) self-raising flour
2 teaspoons baking powder
2 tablespoons cocoa
225g (8oz) unsalted butter, soft
225g (8oz) caster sugar
4 large eggs
For the filling:
500g (1lb) cherries, pitted and 50g
   (2oz) caster sugar OR 400g (14oz)
   cherry conserve (use conserve
   rather than jam as you get more
   whole fruits)
4 teaspoons kirsch
350ml (12floz) double cream
40g (1½oz) dark chocolate

Medlars

The Rude Fruit

Medlars have been cultivated for more than 3,000 years. They probably originated along the west coast of the Caspian Sea, but leaf impressions have been found in interglacial deposits in eastern Germany so they may be one of the ancient trees of Europe. No one is sure, as, in many historical records, 'medlar' referred to any stone fruits.

Medlars were popular with the Greeks and, later, the Romans, who probably brought them to Britain. In medieval times they were regarded as a treat because they ripened late in the season when not much else was available. They were listed as one of the mandatory plants on the royal estates of Charlemagne, and were included in most walled monastery gardens.

Their Latin name, *Mespilus*, comes from the Greek *mesos*, meaning half and *pilos* meaning ball. This refers to the shape of the fruits, which resemble large, squat rosehips. Their shape also earned them the ruder common names of 'open-arse' or 'openars' in England and '*cul-de-chien*' in France. Scotland seems to have been more circumspect with 'how doup' or 'hose doup', meaning hollow berry. In the first edition of *Romeo and Juliet* Shakespeare used '*open et cetera*' in a speech by Mercutio full of double meanings, but this was later changed to '*open-arse*'.

Unless you are going to make jelly with them, medlars need to be 'bletted' or stored to over-ripen before you eat them. This comes from the French term *blessi* which refers to the resulting bruised appearance.

*Now will he sit under
a medlar tree
And wish his mistress
were that kind of fruit
As maids call medlars
when they laugh alone
O Romeo, that she were,
O that she were
An open-arse and thou
a poperin pear!*

Medlar trees are worth growing for their fabulous blossom and wonderful spreading shapes. The fruit is an added, if quirky, bonus.

JANE

The fruits become over-ripe rather than rotten and the flesh soft. The need for them to age has also led to rude jokes regarding age and sex. In Chaucer's *Canterbury Tales*, the Reeve says:

> *But if I fare as dooth an open-ars*
> *That ilke fruyt is ever longer the wers*
> *Til it be roten in mullock or in stree*
> *We old men, I drede, so fare we.*

Which translates as:

> *Unless I be like them there medlar fruit,*
> *Them that gets rottener as they ripen to't,*
> *Till they be rotted down in straw and dung,*
> *That's how we get to be, no longer young.'*
> *Translated by Nevill Coghill, Cresset Press, 1992.*

Medlars had medicinal uses, 'binding the bowels' and, according to Culpeper, easing childbirth and '*making joyful*

Above: The pure white blossom of the medlar tree.
Overleaf: Here the freshly picked medlars (or possibly the closely related hawthorn) are spread out to dry in the sun in northern China.

mothers'. Like many fruits, the seeds are poisonous if eaten in large quantities. Medlars (and the closely related hawthorn with which they are sometimes confused in translation) are commonly used in Chinese medicine; tea made from the pips is said to improve eyesight. The wood is useful as it is very strong and has, over the years, been used for spear points, cudgels and walking sticks. In France, it was also used for the wands of sorcerers, being cut at the first rays of sun at dawn on St John's day.

Ventura is an Italian game using medlars, recorded by scholar Giacomo Castelvetro (1546–1616). It takes place on 10 November, St Martin's Eve, which was when the new wines were sampled. A basket was filled with medlars, three of which had coins embedded in them. The youngest child would take out two fruits for the poor and then everyone would take two in turn. Those who picked the fruits with coins were given money, and the party began with the fruits being eaten with the wine.

There has always been debate as to their desirability in the kitchen. D. H. Lawrence was ambiguous with '*delicious rottenness*', and William Cobbett, the 18th-century writer, was more outspoken with '*It is hardly worth notice, being at best, one degree better than a rotten apple.*' However, 200 years earlier, John Parkinson, the apothecary to James I, referred to the '*pleasant sweetness of them when they are made mellow.*'

The fruits were traditionally stored in damp bran or straw for bletting. In Victorian times the fruits were brought to the table still surrounded by the bran. The pulp was then scooped out, mixed with sugar and cream and eaten as an accompaniment to port. They can also be baked, roasted, stewed with butter or made into wine or cider. It is even possible to make a drink by pouring boiling water over the fruit, but by far the best use is jelly.

Medlar Recipes

900g (2lb) medlars, just ripe but
  not soft; cut into chunks but do
  not peel or deseed; remove any
  damaged or bruised parts
Sufficient water to cover the fruit
  in the pan, about 650ml (22fl oz);
  add more if the fruit is very firm
Juice of one lemon
450g (1lb) granulated sugar,
  depending on the amount of juice

Medlar Jelly

*Beautifully coloured and delicately flavoured, it is
one of the nicest jellies and a perfect partner for toast,
scones and all types of game.*

Add the lemon juice to the water and simmer
until the fruit is soft. Put into a jelly bag and strain
overnight. Do not press the fruit down as this will
make the jelly cloudy. Measure the juice and return
to the pan. For every 600ml (20fl oz) of juice add
450g (1lb) sugar. Heat gently until the sugar has
dissolved and taste for sweetness, adding more
sugar or lemon as necessary. Boil to setting point
(see notes on page 195). Remove from the heat
and clear away any scum. Pour into sterilised jars.
This will make about three small jars of jelly.

Jam-making

Making jam and jelly is perfectly simple and incredibly satisfying, but there are one or two points to be aware of. Unless specified, the instructions below apply to both jam and jelly, even though we have referred only to jam.

Sugar

The type of sugar you use will not alter the taste of the jam but it will affect how it sets. Most importantly, you must always use cane sugar rather than beet. Apparently, in chemical terms, there is no difference between the two, but cane sugar sets much better. If you use beet sugar your preserve will take ages to make and will always be on the runny side.

Whether you use granulated or preserving, refined or unrefined, is entirely up to you. Preserving sugar is more expensive than granulated and not quite so readily available. The individual grains of sugar are larger and this means they dissolve more easily and, in turn, this speeds up the whole process. This is good if, like us, you are impatient, but it doesn't make better jam. Using refined or unrefined sugar is entirely a matter of personal preference. You can get sugar with added pectin to help the jam set but it would not be necessary for any of the fruits in this book as they are all rich in pectin.

Sugar dissolves better if it is warm. Leave the sugar in the packet or pour it into a bowl and put it into a warm oven (150°C/300°F/Gas 2), 30 minutes before you use it.

Setting point

The aspect of jam-making which tends to worry people most is the setting point. This is the point at which the hot bubbling liquid in your pot will set when it cools. It is important not to overcook jam as it can become solid and rubbery and may taste burnt. The important thing to remember is that you can

always cook the jam a bit more, you cannot uncook it. With this in mind, always remove the pot from the heat when you test the jam. This way it will immediately stop cooking. It does not matter how many times you do this, you can even re-cook cold jam if you decide it is not sufficiently set. Testing whether the jam is set is very simple. Before you start, put several saucers into the deep freeze.

When you think the jam may be ready, remove it from the heat and, using a teaspoon, put a small amount of jam onto one of the cold saucers. The jam will rapidly cool. Push your finger through it and, if it forms a wrinkly skin, it means the jam is ready and will set when cooled. The jam is then ready to pour into jars. If it remains runny, replace the pan on the heat and re-test using another cold saucer.

General tips

When cooking the jam, you will probably find a scum forms on the surface. Do not scoop this off while the jam is cooking as you will end up wasting a lot. When making jelly you will need to scoop this off eventually as it will spoil the clarity of the jelly.

Once the jelly has reached setting point, allow it to cool slightly and then scoop off all the scum using a clean spoon. It doesn't look terribly attractive but tastes just as good and can be put in a separate jar and eaten. When making jam you can disperse the scum by adding a little butter. Once the setting point has been reached, put a knob of soft butter into the jam and stir it until it melts. Any scum will miraculously disappear. The amount of butter you need will depend on the quantity of jam you are making and how much scum there is, so start with about ¼ teaspoon and add a little more if necessary.

It is important to sterilise your jars properly otherwise you run the risk of the jam going mouldy. It is perfectly okay to remove any mould and eat the jam below, but it doesn't look very good if you give away a jar of proudly made jam and it has a layer of blue mould on the top. To sterlise, first, heat the oven to 110°C/225°F/Gas ¼. Wash the jars and lids thoroughly in hot, soapy water and rinse well. You can run them through a cycle of a dishwasher if you prefer. Put the jars upside down in the oven and leave them until they are totally dry. If you are using metal lids, they can go in the oven too. Drying the jars in the oven removes the risk of wiping them with a less than spotless cloth, and also means that they are hot and will not crack when you pour the hot jam into them.

When cooking, simmer the fruit slowly to break it up and dissolve the sugar. Then boil it rapidly as the quicker it reaches the setting point the better the flavour will be.

If you want beautiful clear jelly do not press the fruit down into the jelly bag or squeeze it, even if it seems to be dripping through incredibly slowly. Patience really does pay off here, and, if you leave the fruit overnight, all the available juice will drip out.

Mulberries

The Silken Fruit

Like so many other fruits in this book, mulberries originated in Central Asia, spread to Europe along the ancient trade routes, and from there to America. The Romans were probably responsible for introducing them to most European countries, and, by the 16th-century, they were fairly widespread throughout Europe. In Britain, they reached a high point in the early 17th-century thanks to King James I.

Mulberries are often called wise fruits because they only come into bud after any danger of frost has passed. Their Latin name, *Morus*, comes from the word *mora*, meaning delay. Pliny the Elder praised them, and they were dedicated to Minerva, the Roman goddess of wisdom. In the 17th-century, John Evelyn recommended waiting until mulberry leaves appeared to *'bring your oranges etc boldly out of the conservatory'*; the Elizabethan poet, Barnabe Googe, wrote *'when so ever you see the mulberrie begin to spring, you may be sure that winter is at an end.'*

There are four main types of mulberry: black (*Morus nigra*), white (*M. alba*), red (*M. rubra*) and paper (*Broussonetia papyrifera*). The black are the ones to grow for the best fruit but, according to the tale of Pyramus and Thisbe in Ovid's *Metamorphoses*, these fruits were originally white. The two young lovers decided to elope, arranging to meet beneath a mulberry tree. Thisbe arrived first but was frightened by the roar of a lion and ran away, dropping her cloak. The lion, bloodstained from a recent kill, mauled the cloak and then left. Pyramus arrived, was devastated at the death of his love, and stabbed himself to death. His blood stained the tree's roots and the berries turned from white to black. Sadly, the tale ends with Thisbe returning to find her lover dying and killing herself as well.

The fruits of the white mulberry do turn red as they ripen but never develop the same depth of colour or flavour. This is the tree to grow to feed silkworms. Discovered in China in 2500 BC, the manufacture of silk was a closely guarded secret with a death penalty for anyone caught smuggling silkworm eggs or mulberry seeds out of the country. Myths were also spread, including one that the silkworm made its silken cocoon – from which the silk is spun – in the eyebrows of a beautiful maiden. By AD 300–400, the knowledge of how to make silk had spread to India and Japan, but it was ruinously expensive in Europe, selling at its equivalent weight in gold in AD 526. In the 17th-century, James I decided to break this monopoly. He encouraged the planting of mulberry trees the length and breadth of the country, but unfortunately all the trees were black. Although it is possible to make silk from silkworms fed on black mulberries, the white produce the finest silk as the leaves, which the worms eat, appear earlier and are more nutritious. The plan largely failed and many of the plantations became pleasure gardens. The scheme was slightly more successful in the USA where colonists were all given a book on sericulture and required to plant trees, but production was eventually overtaken by cotton. Red mulberries thrive in the USA to this day, even though little silk is made. They are hardier than the black ones and can survive in most of the USA and Canada. They do not do well in the damp, temperate British climate. Both have similar fruits.

The paper mulberry was used to make early paper in China, and lanterns and umbrellas in Japan. The bark fibres were scraped, soaked, beaten and bleached before being mixed with gum and then spread out to dry. Ironing completed the process, which is still carried out today in many parts of rural Japan. When you consider the importance of paper in the spread of knowledge throughout history, the mulberry really does earn its name as the 'wise fruit'.

Mulberries are long-lived, and many of those planted in James I's reign survive today. Sadly, the tree Shakespeare planted at Stratford-upon-Avon no longer exists. In 1752, Rev. Mr Gastrell, who owned the house, cut the tree down as he was bored of showing it to visitors! A tree of a similar age in the Chelsea Physic Garden was dug up during the Second World War to make way for a bomb shelter, but cuttings were taken and many of these have thrived.

Mulberry trees are known to most children, by name if not by looks, from the rhyme *Here We Go Round the Mulberry Bush*. The rhyme describes a number of everyday activities and was one of many similar songs popular throughout Europe in the 19th- and 20th-centuries. It may be a traditional song but the women's prison at Wakefield claims it as its own. There was, and still is, a mulberry tree in the prison yard and legend has it that the women prisoners sang to entertain their children as they exercised round the tree.

Over the years, mulberries have been used for a number of medicinal cures, ranging from syrup for sore throats to aids for digestion. Mulberries have anti-inflammatory properties, and there is even talk of them being used as a future cancer drug. One unusual use is given in the Bible: '*And to the end that they might provoke the elephants to fight, they showed them the blood of grapes and mulberries.*' It is not exactly clear what effect this had.

Above: Bark fibres from the paper mulberry (*Broussonetia papyrifera*) are used to make umbrellas in Japan and ornamental paper in China.
Right: The mulberry tree has inspired a popular nursery rhyme and playground game; *Here We Go Round the Mulberry Bush.*

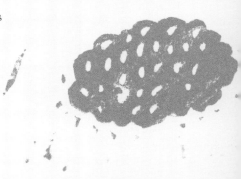

The wood of the tree is hard and attractive and valued
for both cabinetry and fencing. The fruits make a good long-
lasting dye and the leaves can be used to make tea. The juicy
berries are both sweet and tart and are usually eaten simply
with cream. They can be used in any recipe for blackberries
and complement all autumn fruits. The fruits can also be
dried, and, in Afghanistan, the dried berries are powdered
and mixed with flour to make bread.

Mulberry Recipes

Summer Pudding

This is a truly delicious and beautiful pudding.

Serves 4 to 6, depending on greed
850g (2lb) mulberries or mixed
  berries (avoid strawberries because
  they go mushy, and don't use more
  than ⅓ blackcurrants as they will
  overpower the other fruits)
150g (5oz) caster sugar, to taste
7–8 slices day-old white bread,
  crusts removed.

Lightly butter a 900ml (1¾ pint) pudding basin:
the basin's capacity in millilitres should be about
the same as the amount of fruit in grams. Gently
heat the fruit and sugar in a pan, until the sugar
melts. Remove from the heat.

Line the pudding basin tightly with the bread.
Pour the fruit and juice into the bowl, reserving
⅔ of a cup of juice. Cover with a slice of bread, cut
to fit the bowl and press down well. Place a small
plate on top, and put a heavy weight on top. Leave
in the fridge overnight. Turn out, spooning the juice
over any white bits. Serve with cream.

Mulberry Gin

Mulberry gin is one of the easiest home liqueurs to make. It, and the variations below, all turn a fabulous rich purply-red and are ready just in time for Christmas.

Makes about enough for two 70cl bottles, depending on the fruit.

450g (1lb) mulberries

225g (8oz) sugar. How much you need will depend on the fruit and your personal preference. If in doubt add less sugar, you can always taste the liqueur after a month and add a bit more then if it is too bitter.

70cl bottle cheap gin or vodka, if you prefer.

Pick the mulberries when they are ripe and dry and divide them equally between two Kilner or wide-necked screw-top jars. You can make the liqueur in an ordinary bottles but it is a terrible fiddle to get the fruit out.

Add the sugar and then top up each jar with the gin. Close the jars and give them a really good shake to mix everything up. Store in a cool, dark place, shaking or turning the jars regularly. Ideally, this should be every other day but in practice once a week is fine.

Taste a little every month to make sure it is maturing as you want; it should be ready after two or three months.

Strain through a piece of muslin and decant into smaller, pretty bottles. The remaining alcoholic fruit is delicious with ice-cream.

Damson Gin

For this you will need to prick or finely score the skin to release the juice. You can also add one or two almond kernels, cracked, which will give the drink a slight almond flavour.

Sloe Gin

Traditionally, sloes should be individually pricked with a silver pin to release the juice. If this seems like too much of a palaver simply spread the sloes on trays and put in the deep freeze overnight. Sloes will probably need more sugar than mulberries or damsons, possibly as much as an equal amount to the fruit. The left-over fruit is an acquired taste; check you like it before dolloping ice-cream on top.

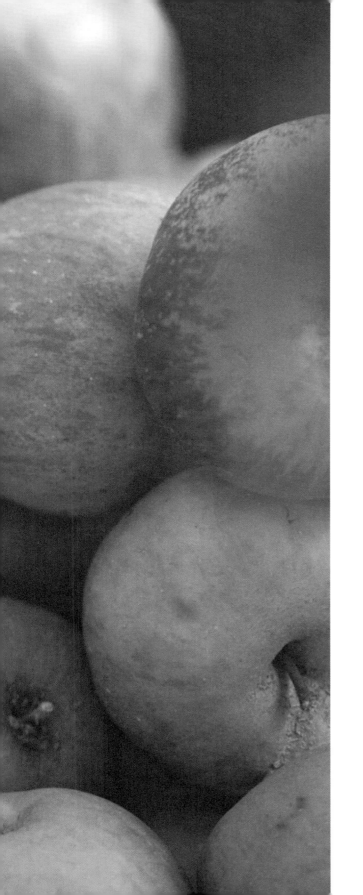

Growing
Fruit Trees

Many people worry about growing their own fruit trees, fearing that it will be incredibly complicated and difficult. This is not really the case, and you can often see overgrown gardens where apple or plum trees continue to thrive and bear large crops of fruit although they have clearly not received any attention for a very long time. All that most orchard fruit requires is a suitable site, enough distance between the trees, some loving care while young, and a little attention afterwards. Many books, written by acknowledged experts, set out with the best intentions but make the whole thing seem unnecessarily complicated.

THE FAMILY TREE

In gardening terms, it is rarely necessary to know the botanical ancestry of a plant, but it is useful as it places each plant in its wider context. The majority of fruits in this book belong to the Rosaceae family, which is one of the largest and also includes roses and hawthorn. Mulberries are the exception, belonging to the Moraceae family. Within the Rosaceae family apples, pears, quinces and medlars are grouped together as pome fruits with a core and pips, whereas plums and cherries have stones. Robert Frost sums it up neatly in his poem *The Rose Family*:

> *This rose is a rose*
> *And was always a rose*
> *But the theory now goes*
> *That the apple's a rose*
> *And the pear is, and so's*
> *The plum, I suppose.*
> *The dear only knows*
> *What will next prove a rose.*

Above: This fence may protect the plant from the prevailing winds and can be used as a support, but it will not provide protection against frost.

Orchard fruits are generally referred to by their common names, but it is worth becoming familiar with the full Latin names so you know exactly what you are getting. Most cultivated apples are generally referred to as *Malus domestica*. Crab apples divide into a number of species and cultivars within the genus, including *M. sylvatica* and *M. baccata*. Pears have developed from *Pyrus communis*. Plums and cherries both fall within the genus *Prunus* – plums, including greengages, classified as *P. domestica*, sour or acid cherries as *P. cerasus* and sweet cherries, *P. avium*. Further relations of the plum are damsons, Mirabelles and bullaces (varieties of *P. institia*) and sloes (*P. spinosa*). Quinces are *Cydonia oblonga*, medlars *Mespilus germanica*, and mulberries *Morus nigra* (black) or *M. alba* (white) according to whether you want fruit or silk. The flowering quince, or japonica, is *Chaenomeles*.

Hybridisation and selective breeding has led to thousands of cultivars around the world. Rather than the full Latin name, they are often simply referred to by the cultivar name, e.g. the pear Conference or the apple Bramley's Seedling.

SITE
You may not have much choice where to plant your fruit trees but it is worth knowing what they like so you can modify the existing conditions if necessary.

Climate
Most of northern Europe and North America have perfect climates for growing fruit trees. In northerly or exposed areas or high altitudes you may need the protection of a wall. Note that it needs to be a wall to provide the extra warmth; wooden fences do not retain heat in the same way.

If climate change increases winter warmth it hinders some varieties of apples, pears and plums, which need a number of

cold days in winter to form good fruit buds. On the other hand, greengages will probably thrive if the temperature rises slightly and many fruits will not mind either way.

Frost at blossom time can be a problem, with pears and plums being most at risk because they flower early. Plant these trees in the most sheltered spots, and, if they are small protect them with fleece when necessary. If you are worried about frost, plant late-flowering or resistant varieties.

Position
A sunny, sheltered site suits most fruit trees. Morello cherries thrive in shade, and medlars and some plums (Czar and Victoria) don't mind a certain amount. Damsons, bullaces, sloes and crab apples will all cope with being buffeted, so these can be used as windbreaks if necessary.

Above: This brick wall provides a strong support to train the tree against and will also provide protection against frost. During the day, the bricks absorb and store heat which they then release in the evening, providing a micro-climate of warmer air.

Soil

All fruit trees like moist, well-drained, fertile soil. A pH of
6.5–7 is ideal. Quinces, plums and pears on quince rootstock
like damper but not waterlogged conditions. If you are growing
on a large scale it may be worth installing a drainage system.
On a smaller scale, if you have heavy clay, add lots of grit and
organic matter to improve the drainage. Conversely, if your
soil is very light and sandy, incorporate organic matter
so the water and nutrients will not be lost.

CHOOSING AND PLANNING

The size and number of trees you plant will obviously be
governed by the amount of space you have and your personal
preferences – but there are a couple of points you must take
into account if you want your fruit trees to do well.

Pollination

For fertilization to occur and the tree to grow fruit, the right
pollen needs to get from one flower to another. Bees and other
insects, along with the wind, all help in the transfer. Growing
bee-friendly plants nearby will make this easier. To set fruit,
most apples, most sweet cherries, many pears and some plums
need fertilizing with pollen from one or more *different* varieties
of the same species (a crab apple will do fine for most apples).
Obviously, both trees need to be in flower at the same time.
Remember that any suitable tree within 18m (60ft) will do,
so those in neighbouring gardens may help. Quinces, medlars
and most mulberries are self-fertile, which means they do not
need a pollination partner. Elaborate pollination tables exist to
show which varieties are compatible. However, there is a much
easier solution. Simply ask for the help of an experienced fruit
nurseryman when you are buying your trees and you should
be properly advised.

Right: Bees are one of the most important pollinators of fruit trees. The pollen sticks to their legs and is carried from flower to flower around the orchard.

Rootstocks

Most orchard fruit trees consist of two compatible parts grafted or joined together, one above ground and one below. The rootstock, the below-ground portion, will determine the tree's final size, depending slightly on how vigorous the variety is and local conditions, such as soil and aspect. It may also influence disease-resistance and hardiness. The top or tree part will determine the variety of fruit you get. Always check the rootstock: if the garden centre or nursery can't tell you what it is, don't buy the tree. Everyone knows what a full-sized tree looks like but when you get down to descriptions such as dwarfing, very dwarfing and extremely dwarfing, different people have different ideas as to the exact size – but the rootstock provides a firm guide.

Rootstocks may be identified either by names or numbers. The slightly confusing references for apples refer to the research stations where they were first developed (M: Malling, MM: Merton Malling), and the order in which they were developed.

As a general rule, the more dwarfing the rootstock, the more care the plant will need throughout its life, in terms of nutrition, watering and weeding. Small rootstocks need very good soil, but in return they will flower and fruit a year or so earlier. Most trees will fruit within three to four years, but very vigorous rootstocks may take six to seven; very dwarf trees will begin in their second or third year. The chart opposite gives the most common rootstocks. You may find others in nurseries, but these should give you a good base to work from. The sizes refer to the rough height and spread of a freestanding tree.

Medlars are usually grown on hawthorn or quince rootstock. If you have moist soil, quince is better. They will eventually reach 3.6–6m (12–20ft) depending on the variety and site. Mulberries reach 6–10m (20–30ft). Both are usually wider than they are tall.

Size	Apple	Pear	Plum	Cherry	Quince
Very vigorous 7.5–10m/ 25–30ft	M25	Pyrus communis	Brompton Myrobalan B	Malling F12/1	–
Vigorous 5.5–7m/ 18–22ft	MM111	–	–	–	–
Semi-vigorous (Semi-dwarfing) 4.5–5.5m/15–18ft	MM106	QA or BA29	St Julien A	Colt	QA
Semi-dwarfing (Dwarfing) 3–3.5m/10–15ft	M26	QC	Pixy	Gisela 5 or Damil	–
Dwarfing (Very dwarfing) 2–3m/8–10ft	M9	–	–	–	–
Very dwarfing (Extremely dwarfing) 1.5–2m/5–6ft	M27	–	–	–	–

Rootstocks for different tree shapes
Different rootstocks are especially suited for particular shapes of tree. Examples for apples are shown below:
Standard: M25, MM111 (1.8m/6ft clear trunk)
Half standard: MM111, MM106 (1.4m/4ft clear trunk)
Espalier, fan: MM111, MM106, M26
Cordon: M9, M27
Step-over: M27

For trees in containers, choose M26 – the container will restrict the size anyway, and these rootstocks are better able to cope with the stresses of growing in a pot.

Fans and espaliers need to be grown on a fairly vigorous rootstock so they can form the framework.

Spacing

The spacings between your trees will depend on the rootstock
and how you want to train the plant. As a general rule, the
branches of different trees should not touch once they are
fully grown. Work out the final spread of the trees and allow
a few feet extra between each one. Cordons should be planted
at least 60cm (2ft) apart. This amount of space means the
air circulates better and your trees will be healthier as pests
and diseases will find it harder to take hold.

Tip and spur-bearing varieties

Most apples are spur-bearing, which means that the fruit
buds are formed on spurs along the side branches. Tip-bearing
varieties bear the fruits at the ends of their branches. Medlars
and some pears are also tip-bearing. Tip-bearers cannot be
used for trained shapes as you would be constantly cutting
off the productive ends.

BUYING

A fruit tree will be around for a long time, so it is worth
buying from a specialist nursery or garden centre, you really
trust. The tree should be a good balanced shape and appear
healthy, with leaves or buds according to the season. Check
the graft looks firm, with no cracking around the join, and
that it is above the level of the soil.

Young trees will settle in more quickly and be better in the
long run. A one-year-old tree is called a maiden or whip and will
have no side shoots. A feathered maiden is two years old and
will have the beginnings of side branches forming. Three years
old is about the maximum you should buy, as many trees start
to flower and fruit in their fourth year and should be settled
in their final growing place by then. If you want trained shapes
you can buy trees which have been formatively pruned to point
their branches in the right directions and get you started.

Above: Sensible spacing between these trees allows air to circulate and gives easy access to the fruit.

Whether you buy bare-rooted or containerised plants doesn't really matter, and will probably depend on your supplier. Just remember, bare-rooted trees need to go into the ground immediately whereas plants in containers won't mind waiting a few days. To avoid the use of pesticides and other chemicals, try to choose disease-resistant varieties.

PLANTING

Fruit trees are best planted in late autumn or early winter (depending on the climate you are in). This ensures the soil is not too cold and gives the plant time to get established before it has to worry about putting on new growth in the spring. Do not plant a fruit tree in exactly the same place as a previous one.

Choose a day when the soil is not waterlogged or frozen. Dig a hole large enough to accommodate the roots when they are spread out. If the soil is very compacted, break it up.

Fix a stake so it will be on the windward side of the trunk. Containerised plants need an angled stake so you do not disturb the root ball. It should form an angle of 45 degrees, with the ground on the windward side.

Sprinkle some bonemeal into the hole and settle the tree in, ensuring the graft union is above ground level. Firm in and water well. Fix the tree to the stake using tree ties or soft twine which will not damage the tree as it grows. You should then mulch with organic matter, leaving a gap around the trunk to stops it rotting. Mulching stop weeds growing, conserves water and feeds the tree.

CARE

For the first three to four years, all fruit trees will benefit from a little care. You should water the trees regularly to ensure they don't dry out and feed and mulch them in spring. Check the ties every few months to ensure they are not getting too tight.

Right: This stake is perfect to support a newly planted bare-rooted tree. A container-grown plant would need an angled stake so as not to disturb the root ball. Ties should always be loose enough to allow room for growth.

Stakes on standards and half standards can usually be removed after two years. Shake the tree gently to check whether the roots are firm. Always remove stakes in early spring at the start of the growing season, to give the tree time to adjust while the weather is mild. Hard as it may seem, you should remove the blossom the first spring after planting, so the tree can concentrate on settling into its new home rather than producing fruit. For the same reason, the ground around the trunk should be kept clear of grass and weeds for the first couple of years. Plum trees are very fussy about any competition for water and nutrients, and the surrounding soil should be kept clear until they are well established. Trees on dwarfing rootstocks will always need a clear area, roughly equal to the diameter of the canopy.

Heavy crops on apples, pears and plums should be thinned throughout the summer, cutting off any rotting, diseased or damaged fruit at the same time. The June Drop will get rid of some surplus fruits naturally but you will probably need to continue the process, especially on young trees. You should leave one or two fruits per cluster and aim for 10cm (6in) between cooking apples and pears, 7.5cm (3in) between plums and dessert apples. It is tempting to leave all the fruits in place and go for a huge crop, but the resulting fruits will be small and the tree will be exhausted and may not crop so well the following year. You then run the risk of the trees becoming biennial bearing, which means it only bears fruit every other year (see Glossary).

All fruit trees will benefit from being mulched with well-rotted organic matter in spring and autumn. Plums should be fed with lime in late winter to help the stones form within the fruits. Simply apply crushed limestone around the base and water in. Pears require a good supply of water from the moment the buds open and then for six weeks after flowering. If the weather is dry, give each tree a bucket of water every day.

Mulberries are also thirsty trees. All this will give you a better harvest and healthier trees but, in reality, most trees will manage well on their own once mature.

Fruit trees in containers
Many fruit trees do well in containers, but they need constant care throughout their lives. The final pot should be at least 45cm (18in) wide and deep. Put drainage holes and crocks in the bottom of any pot and use specialist compost (John Innes No. 3 is good), or multipurpose compost with one third grit or perlite added. You can also add moisture-retaining gel. These can be bought at garden centres and other suppliers and consist of granules that swell up and hold water. This is then gradually released into the soil, which means the plant gets a constant supply of water. You still have to water, just not so often. In cold weather, when there is a danger of frost, you

should lag the pot to prevent the compost freezing. Drape plastic, fleece or newspaper loosely around it and tie in place. This will trap slightly warmer air around the pot and should prevent it, and the soil, freezing. If you buy a container-grown tree, do not put it straight into the large pot but gradually increase the size over a number of years. This will encourage the tree to grow slowly. Once the tree is in its final container, the compost should be partly renewed every couple of years. Wait until the leaves have dropped, prune the roots if necessary, and replace one third of the compost with fresh.

Regular maintenance is the most important thing for all container plants, especially constant supplies of water and nutrients. Never let them dry out in summer or become soggy in winter. Feed regularly – a high potassium liquid tomato food every fortnight during the growing season is ideal. Remember if you grow flowers or herbs in the same container you will need to provide proportionately more food and water.

PRUNING

For most people, this is the scariest part of fruit growing – how much to cut off and when to cut it. It actually matters much less than you might think, and many trees will crop perfectly well without being pruned at all. Even if you do cut too much, the worst that will probably happen is that you will reduce your harvest for a year. Obviously, if you are going to train your trees you will need expert advice or a specialist book. For ordinary trees, once they are fully grown, all you need to do is cut off the Three Ds (dead, diseased and damaged branches) and ensure that as much light and air as possible reaches all parts of the tree by removing crossing or inward-growing branches.

Pruning should be carried out in either summer or winter, depending on the fruit and the results you want. Summer pruning will restrict growth and is most useful when training plants. Winter pruning stimulates growth and is important for

establishing the framework of the tree. All trees store energy in late summer and early autumn. If you reduce the amount of foliage before this time the tree will store less energy and will grow with correspondingly less vigour the following spring. If you do not prune the tree until winter it will have stored the maximum amount of energy and will put on more new growth in spring.

For the first three to four years you need to build up a good balanced framework. Upright growth will make the tree bigger and stronger but the lateral branches are the ones that will give you fruit. Most branches should have two types of bud. Fruit buds are plump, round and stick up, and will develop into the following year's fruit. Wood buds are slender and pointy and grow at a leaf axil, the point where a leaf grows out from the main stem. These will form new branches. Once you have established the basic shape, pruning is simply a matter of maintaining a healthy tree and keeping a balance of old and new wood.

Use winter pruning on all young trees, except plums and cherries, to remove crossing stems and any that are too low. Cut back to where the branch meets a larger branch or the trunk. Do not cut back too much otherwise you will end up with a lot of strong, straight, leafy growth rather than the twiggy branches which bear fruit buds. Water shoots are tall vigorous shoots that grow straight up, usually in the centre of the tree. Most should be removed unless you want a new branch where one is growing.

Summer pruning is best carried out in mid- to late summer when the plant has stopped growing. Work out which are the main branches. Each branch growing out from these needs to be pruned. At the base of each shoot there will be a tight cluster of leaves – this is the basal cluster. Count three leaves up from this cluster and cut the stem just above the third leaf. Side shoots growing from these shoots need to be cut back to one leaf above the basal cluster. This method will ensure the tree does not put on too much new, unproductive growth and will give you blossom and fruit right along the branches.

There are one or two special considerations. Tip-bearers should not be pruned much as you will be removing the fruiting tips. If necessary, reduce the leader of each branch by a third and cut any laterals so that five or six buds remain on the branch.

Plums and cherries should be pruned as little as possible and only on a dry day in early to mid-summer to reduce the risk of silver leaf – a serious disease. The spores of silver leaf are dormant in summer and the rising sap of the tree will make it more resistant. Carry out the formative pruning of young trees in early spring.

Pears and quinces should be treated as apples. They will continue to fruit if left unpruned but the fruits may get very small if left alone.

Medlars rarely need pruning. They fruit at the tips, so any you remove will reduce your harvest.

Mulberries need little pruning. Diseased and damaged branches should be removed in winter.

PROBLEMS

Fruit trees are prone to a variety of diseases, but many can be avoided by choosing resistant varieties and keeping your trees healthy. Ensure there is good air circulation and always remove any diseased or damaged branches. Make sure the soil drains well, especially in winter, and clear away fallen leaves. Unwanted insects can be caught in sticky traps hanging from the branches or by putting grease bands around the trunk. These can be bought from specialist suppliers. Vigorous, healthy trees will be able to fight off most problems. Creating a diversity of plants, both within the fruits and around them, will add to the general health of the garden.

Right: The band of grease on this trunk will protect the tree from coddling moth.

NATURE'S OWN DEFENCE

Certain plants can be used to help keep your trees healthy
naturally. Some of these companion plants will help fight
diseases; others will attract helpful predators such as
ladybirds, hoverflies and lacewings that will eat some of the
pests threatening your crop. There is much debate as to how
much good companion planting does, but one thing is certain
– it does no harm. Mixed planting around your trees, whether
of wild or garden flowers or herbs will make the whole area
healthier, and more interesting to look at. Bees and birds will
also be attracted; your trees will be well pollinated and alive
with birdsong. Try to mix your planting as much as you can and
alter it a little each year so the soil does not become worn out.

Some of the most useful plants

Chives (*Allium schoenoprasum*) will help against mildew
and blackspot and have pretty purple or white flowers in
summer. They are also delicious in salads and sandwiches.
Tansy (*Tanacetum vulgare*) will deter fruit moths and is a
perennial with bright yellow button-shaped flowers in summer.
Penstemons and nasturtiums (*Tropaeolum majus*) will
discourage woolly aphids and, with a little training, the
nasturtiums will scramble up any low branches. Gaillardias,
poached egg flower (*Limnanthes douglasii*), phacelia, pot
marigolds (*Calendula*) and cow parsley (*Anthriscus sylvestris*)
all attract beneficial insects, are easy to grow and will look
great around the base of your trees. The Allium genus will
deter pests and attract beneficial insects. The taller ones look
particularly lovely beneath the trees in early summer. French
marigolds (*Tagetes*) and herbs such as rosemary, thyme,
sage and lavender deter predators by disorientating them
or masking the scent of the fruit with their own fragrance.
If the shade isn't too dense you can make a herb garden
around your trees.

Encouraging wildlife and beneficial insects does not mean you have to let your garden run wild – in fact, a reasonably tidy garden is actually healthier. Fragrant flowers nearly all attract wildlife, single flowers are usually more attractive than the doubles or hybrids as they tend to have less pollen. Leaving some windfalls on the ground will provide valuable winter food for birds and animals. Once you have attracted the insects at the bottom of the food chain, everything else will naturally follow.

Plants to attract butterflies and beneficial insects
Buddleja (*Buddleja davidii*), cornflower (*Centaurea*), forget-me-not (*Myosotis*), lavender, marigolds (*Tagetes*), Michaelmas daisy (*Aster*), Oriental poppy (*Papaver orientale*), phlox, pinks (*Dianthus*), red valerian (*Centranthus ruber*), scabious (*Scabiosa*), sedum, tobacco plant (*Nicotiana*), violas and most herbs.

Below: These pink cornflowers will make your orchard look pretty. They will also attract butterflies and beneficial insects.

In the 1950s, all the boys used to go scrumping for fruit. The farmers hated us. One was said to load his cartridges with rock salt, which would draw blood on bare legs but not put you in hospital. We never dared find out if it was true. CHRIS

Creating a meadow in your orchard

Allowing the grass to grow a little longer and encouraging wild flowers will create a beautiful and natural surround for your orchard. However, there are one or two points to remember. Firstly, meadows thrive on poor soil, whereas your fruit trees need reasonably rich soil, so you will have to achieve a balance. Most fruit trees, especially plums, do not like too much competition immediately above their roots, so it pays to keep the grass around the trunk slightly shorter.

The easiest way to introduce meadow flowers is to plant plugs or small plants, but this can work out very expensive if you are covering a large area. In practice, it is usually best to use a mixture of plugs and seed mixtures, which you can scatter in spring. You can buy ready mixed seeds which will give you a good balance of plants and are available for different soils. Typical plants are: campion (*Silene*), cornflower (*Centaurea*), love-in-a-mist (*Nigella*), meadow cranesbill (*Geranium pratense*) and poppies (*Papaver*).

Planting bulbs within the grass is also a good idea. Crocus, snake's head fritillaries, dwarf narcissus and snowdrops (*Galanthus*) will all provide colour and attract insects early in the year before the grass and wild flowers grow too tall.

In late summer you should cut the long areas back, first with a strimmer or shears and then with a mower on a high setting. This fits with the cycle of the fruit trees as all but the earliest can be harvested with short grass underfoot. It is worth maintaining some paths of shorter grass through your meadow throughout the summer for easy access and direction. Always rake up grass clippings so they do not form a solid mat when it rains.

Using chemicals will upset the natural balance of your orchard, may harm wildlife, and seems ludicrous when you are gong to eat the crop. Many problems, such as pear rust, look much worse than they are and will not seriously harm your fruit. If in doubt, ask the nursery where you bought the tree or a gardening advisory body such as the Royal Horticultural Society.

SOME COMMON DISEASES

Canker – affects all tree fruits and is worst on poor, badly drained soil. Make sure your soil is in tip-top condition, adding lots of grit if necessary and topping up with a nutritious mulch in spring and autumn.

Scab – this is worst in mild, wet weather. Cut and burn badly affected stems and always clear away fallen leaves in winter.

Plum blossom wilt – this fungus enters via the flowers, which then wilt and die. Cut off any affected flowers immediately. This will reduce your harvest but the tree shouldn't suffer any long-term harm.

Silver leaf – this affects plums and cherries but can largely be avoided by pruning only in summer when the spores are dormant and the tree's sap is rising.

Brown rot – commonly affects quinces; cut away affected fruit and rake away leaves in autumn.

Fireblight – this is a bacterial disease which may affect any fruit tree. Cut away and burn affected branches and disinfect pruning tools to stop it spreading. In severe cases you may lose the whole tree.

Left: The paper around these pears protects them and ensures that each fruit is kept apart from its neighbour. This way, mould and diseases are less likely to spread.

Above: Medlars 'bletting' in sand. Fruit can be stored in plastic bags as long as you allow air to circulate.

OTHER PROBLEMS

Biennial bearing can affect apples and pears. If a tree has a very large crop one year it may become exhausted and bear no fruit the following year. It then regains its strength and bears another huge crop the year after, often of tiny fruits. To prevent or break this cycle so that you get regular crops each year, remove some of the fruits during the summer, when the fruits begin to form. As a rough guide, leave about half the fruits or one per cluster, depending on how they grow. Prune lightly in summer, cutting any long, new growth back to three to four buds.

Birds can be a pest, and if you have small or trained cherries it may be worth netting them. Otherwise it is probably worth losing a few fruits in return for birdsong in your orchard.

Wasps are most hazardous when you are harvesting as they feast on ripe and rotting fruit. You can lure them into special traps or just be careful.

Moths can cause damage but this can usually be avoided if you put greasebands around the trunk and any supporting posts in early autumn – this will deter the caterpillars from climbing up.

Aphids can be a problem, especially with plums which are especially vulnerable. Their leaves may curl up in an unsightly and alarming manner in spring. This is less serious than it looks and will not harm the fruits or the tree.

HARVESTING

When you harvest your fruit will depend on both the type of fruit and the individual variety. Amounts and times will vary from year to year. Always pick fruit on a dry day as it will keep better. Apples are ripe when the fruit comes away from the stem when the fruit is gently lifted and twisted. Do not pull down or tear it away. Pears are ready when they 'give' slightly when lightly pressed near the stalk. They should still be fairly firm as they ripen from the centre outwards – so by the time the outside is soft, the inside will have turned to mush. Plums, cherries and mulberries will be just tender to touch; squeeze them very gently to avoid bruising the fruit. Another, delightful, way to test is to eat fruit straight from the tree. The easiest way to harvest mulberries is to spread sheets around the tree and shake the branches. Quinces remain rock hard but should be golden and aromatic and come away from the stem easily. Medlars are ready to harvest in late autumn and can be made into jelly straight away. If you are going to eat them they need to be 'bletted' (stored until soft).

Cherries are the first to crop, usually ready in mid-summer, with mulberries soon after. Plums follow in early autumn, with greengages and damsons first and finally bullaces and sloes. Pears are ready from early autumn onwards. Apples can be harvested as early as mid-summer or as late as Christmas. The final fruits to harvest are quinces and medlars in mid- to late autumn. Whatever you do, harvest slowly and gently, and enjoy it. This is the result of all your labours and should provide you with fruit for weeks or even months. Be proud of it!

Left: A view towards the apple house at West Dean in Sussex which has some of the finest orchard fruit in Britain.

STORING

Use windfalls immediately, cutting away any bruised or damaged flesh. There is nothing wrong with these fruits but they will not store.

For all fruits, a cool, outdoor storeroom is ideal, the main requirements being that it is dark, airy, frost-free and safe from pests. A reasonable level of humidity will stop the fruits drying out and going wrinkly. Do not store strong-smelling things such as creosote or onions in the same area as the fruit will absorb the odours. Temperatures in attics tend to fluctuate too much.

The fruits should be stored slightly apart from their neighbours so that if one rots the others will not be affected. Slatted shelves, fruit trays or shallow boxes are all perfect. Thin stockings hung from rafters are also good. They may look strange hanging down, but they allow the air to circulate and you can easily spot any rotting fruit. Clear plastic bags can be used to store fruit in 2–3kg (4–6lb) batches with pinpricks punched in the bags to allow air circulation. Always label the different varieties and check once a week to remove any rotting fruit.

As a general rule, late dessert apples store better than early varieties. Most cookers store well. Both apples and pears should be picked slightly under-ripe as they will continue to ripen in storage. Pears need to be checked regularly as they only last a few days once ripe. Medlars will store for two to three weeks with the eye facing downwards and quinces for two to three months. Keep a few quinces in a bowl indoors to get the benefit of their wonderful scent. Plums, cherries and mulberries are best eaten straight away or preserved.

You can freeze, purée, preserve or dry fruit. Pressing to make juice is another option. All alcoholic drinks store well: wine for a few months, cider longer and liqueurs many years.

Resources

Varieties to Choose

APPLES

There are hundreds of interesting apples you could consider growing; whichever we suggest we are bound to have left out somebody's favourite. The list is split into two parts. The first consists of four fairly reliable, easily available and good-tasting apples with which you might want to get started. The second contains some heritage varieties chosen for their taste but which may well not be easy for everyone to cultivate. Even where an apple is described as self-fertile you will still get a better crop if there are other suitable apples (crabs included) nearby.

Queen Cox is probably the apple to grow if you like the taste of Cox's Orange Pippin but have been put off by its reputation of being tricky to grow. It has a wonderful red colour and a very Coxy taste. It is generally said to be self-fertile.

Bramley is still by far the most popular cooking apple, even though it requires two pollination partners, makes a big tree, and can have various problems. However, the flesh melts down to a wonderful fluff when cooked, and it maintains high levels of acidity even when stored. Try to get the tree on a M9 rootstock to restrict its size.

Egremont Russet is, if you like the slightly nutty taste of russet apples, one of the best. It is said by some nurseries to be self-fertile and is relatively easy to grow, although not totally trouble-free (it sometimes suffers from bitter pit – check your soil is right).

Greensleeves was first introduced in 1966 and is a very easy apple with a golden colour and a sweet taste. It is an excellent all rounder and usually said to be self-fertile. This and Queen Cox are two of the easiest apples to grow and would represent a good starting point for most beginners to orchard fruit.

Heritage varieties

It is best to seek further advice from an established nurseryman to find which variety will suit your site. When selecting, try to provide as much information as you can to get the right match for you and your needs. A little time spent here will ensure many years of pleasure.

Orleans Reinette tastes delicious with a crisp texture and nutty flavour; but not high yielding nor a good keeper once picked. Prone to biennial bearing.

Blenheim Orange is perhaps the best of all the heritage varieties and will even grow in northern England. A high-yielding dual purpose apple, whose only major problems are a tendency to scab and biennial bearing.

Ashmead's Kernel is arguably the best-tasting eating apple available, but it is difficult to get it to bear a decent crop of fruit; it tends to develop bitter pit in some soils. The fruit generally keeps very well.

Newton Wonder is a very good juicy cooker with sufficient acid. It boils down to a wonderful golden fluff. It is, however, a fairly large tree and prone to biennial bearing.

Catshead is one of the best-tasting cooking apples and has the distinctive shape its name implies. Stock is difficult to source and, for all its qualities, it is one for the enthusiast.

PEARS

Some pears are very tolerant about their growing conditions, others much fussier. We have given a section of both below:

Doyenné du Comice is the ultimate for taste and texture but a fussy tree that requires perfect conditions.

Conference is a tough, reliable variety; it is self-fertile but produces a better crop with a partner. The fruit stores well and can be used for dessert or cooking.

Concorde is a cross between Conference and Doyenné du Comice, with good qualities from both.

Catillac is a cooker with good flavour; it turns an attractive pink when cooked. Vigorous tree with reliable, heavy crops. Triploid.

Louise Bonne of Jersey has deliciously flavoured fruit. The trees crop well and are partially self-fertile.

QUINCES
Nearly all the available varieties of quince are relatively modern and there is not much to choose between them, given the utterly beautiful blossom and golden-green fruits produced by each variety. Meech's Prolific is a relatively high yielder while both Vranja and Champion have their advocates. Other varieties are available from some sources but are less common.

PLUMS
The two best eating and general purpose plums are Victoria and Marjorie's Seedling, both of which are moderately self-fertile and produce good-tasting fruit (also good for cooking in most recipes) in reasonable abundance. Although not totally problem-free, they are both fairly easy and will give a lot of pleasure to their owners.

Merryweather is generally considered to be the best damson. It is self-fertile, tough, and should give few problems as well as providing excellent fruit.

You may be lucky and find a UK supplier of Mirabelle plums if you want to cook tarte aux Mirabelles (most are in the Lorraine area of France where the trees are traditionally grown, although they would probably be hardy in southern England). The best greengage, in our opinion, is probably the Cambridge Gage with juicy yellowish-green fruit. It is partially self-fertile.

Overleaf: (Left) Cox's Orange Pippin apple; (Right) Meech's Prolific quince.

CHERRIES

The cherries here may seem to be the commonest varieties but there is a reason: they all reliably produce really tasty fruit.

Stella is self-fertile with sweet, red, juicy fruits. Compact Stella forms a smaller tree.

Sunburst is self-fertile with sweet, black fruits.

Morello is a self-fertile acid cherry that is almost unique in the fruit world for thriving in shade.

Mayduke has sharp fruits that have good flavour. The trees are compact, partially self-fertile and will crop in semi-shade.

MEDLARS

All are self-fertile. As a general rule, larger trees will give you larger fruits.

Dutch and **Monstrous** are spreading trees that crop well and have large flowers in spring and large, well-flavoured fruits.

Nottingham and **Royal** are compact trees with smaller fruits.

MULBERRIES

All are self-fertile and are often sold simply as the species. This will give you a medium-sized tree with good fruits. **Chelsea** is a good variety of black mulberry with large fruits that ripen early.

Gardens to Visit

This is a small selection of gardens with orchards or collections of fruit trees. We have chosen those which we particularly like and there are obviously many more. Many of the gardens have other features of interest. Most are open for a reasonable season each year, but it is always worth checking beforehand.

ENGLAND
London Area
Barge Gardens, 31 Mill St, SE1 2AX.
These are part of the National Gardens Scheme and are only open for a few days each year, but are really worth visiting if you can. The 'garden' consists of seven barges moored on the River Thames just below Tower Bridge. There are medlars, crab apples, an avenue of quinces and amazing views of London.

Fenton House, Hampstead Grove, Hampstead, NW3 6SP.
Tel 020 7435 3471 (National Trust)
This contains a small orchard, dating from the 17th-century, which has been restored. In spring there is a carpet of bulbs and in summer there are mown paths through the long grass. There are Apple Day celebrations.

Fulham Palace, Bishops Avenue, Fulham Palace Road, SW6 6EA.
Tel 020 7736 3233 (www.fulhampalace.org)
This was the Bishop of London's palace from the 11th-century until 1973. The original orchards were created by Bishop FitzJames (1506–22), and were described in 1647 as

'*orchards walled in brick*'. A gate and part of the wall survive, but the orchard now stretches away from the palace rather than towards it, in a walled garden created in the 18th-century. Fruit trees line the central path forming a long arch. In one quarter an apple orchard has been planted around bee hives using varieties that were traditionally grown at the palace. Spreading out from the beautiful restored vinery, there is a knot garden, working kitchen garden and pergola with a magnificent wisteria. The orchard will take time to mature but this is a perefect example of how a garden can be successfully revitalised. (Quote taken from *A Walk Round Fulham Palace and Its Garden* by Sibella Jane Flower for the Friends of Fulham Palace 2002.)

Southside House, Woodhayes Road, Wimbledon Common, SW19 4RJ.

Tel 020 8946 7643 (www.southsidehouse.com)
Home of the Munthe family, this opens as part of the London Open Garden Squares weekend but is also open regularly throughout the summer. There is a small and very charming orchard set amidst a wildflower meadow, which is especially beautiful in spring.

Buckinghamshire
Hughenden Manor, High Wycombe, HP14 4LA.
Tel 01494 755573 (National Trust)
The Victorian walled kitchen garden has 50 varieties of old apples, and there are Morello cherries trained against walls. A new orchard was planted in the 1990s with local varieties. There are Apple Day celebrations.

Cheshire

Little Moreton Hall, Congleton, CW12 4SD.
Tel 01260 272018 (National Trust)
This is a 15th-century house surrounded by a 20th-century garden, but the two work well together. The orchard leads straight off the cobbled courtyard and is a mixture of old and new trees. One of the bigger pear trees has a wonderful rambler rose trailing through it.

The Walled Garden, Norton Priory, Tudor Road, Manor Park, Runcorn, WA7 1SX.
Tel 01928 569895 (www.nortonpriory.org)
The national collection of quinces (*Cydonia*) is in an old walled garden attached to the ruins of a medieval priory. Do not be put off by the approach through an industrial estate – the priory and garden are lovely. There is a Quince Festival in October.

Derbyshire

Hardwick Hall, Doe Lea, Chesterfield, S44 5QJ.
Tel 01246 850430 (National Trust and English Heritage)
Much of the garden is divided into courts, and the South
Court covers an amazing seven-and-a-half acres. It is neatly
divided into quarters with orchards in two, specimen trees
in a third and a fabulous herb garden in the fourth. One of the
best views is from the upper landing of the house, where you
can fully appreciate the scale and pattern. The south-east
orchard has apples, pears, plums, gages and damsons, while
that in the north-east has old varieties including crab apples
in long grass with naturalised daffodils and wildflowers.

Devon

**Royal Horticultural Society Garden, Rosemoor, Great
Torrington, EX38 8PH.**
Tel 01805 624067 (www.rhs.org.uk)
The orchard here is not on the same scale as the one at RHS
Wisley, but it is planted with local varieties which is useful if
you want to know which ones will do well in the area. There
is also a large walled garden with fruit and vegetables.

Essex

Audley End, Saffron Walden, CB11 4JF.
Tel 01799 522842 (www.english-heritage.org.uk)
The two-acre kitchen garden dates from the 1750s and has
been in use almost continuously. It has been authentically
restored by English Heritage, using predominantly pre-1900
plants, and is run by Garden Organic. There are beautifully
trained fruit trees and an orchard house. Before you visit,
try to read the *The Diary of a Victorian Gardener* by William
Cresswell, who worked there in 1874.

Gloucestershire

Westbury Court, Westbury-on-Severn, GL14 1PD.
Tel 01452 760461 (National Trust)

Westbury Court is interesting as it is the only Dutch-style
William and Mary garden to survive intact in England. The
espaliered fruit trees are grown as much for ornamentation
as production and are all pre-1700 varieties, including the
apples Court Pendu Plat and Catshead and the pears
Bellissime d'Hiver, Catillac and Black Worcester. Some,
such as the pear Beurre Brown, can hardly be seen anywhere
else. A bright carpet of bulbs contrasts beautifully with the
blossom in spring, and in autumn the coloured fruits look
very striking.

Hereford and Worcester

Berrington Hall, nr Leominster, HR6 0DW.
Tel 01568 615721 (National Trust)

The Walled Garden was replanted in the 1980s with patterns
of fruit trees including medlars and mulberries. Within the
grassy areas there are 50 varieties of apple, most pre-1900
and many local to Herefordshire. They are on MM106
rootstock so you can walk easily beneath them – a luxury
we rarely get nowadays.

Hergest Croft, Kington, HR5 3EG.
Tel 01544 230160 (www.hergest.co.uk)

The old-fashioned kitchen garden has a beautiful avenue of
wonderfully ancient, twisted, apple trees. Beneath these there
are a succession of bulbs; daffodils are followed by grape
hyacinths and tulips. There is also an orchard linking the
kitchen garden to the house.

Hertfordshire

Hatfield House, Hatfield, AL9 5HX.
Tel 01707 287010 (www.hatfield-house.co.uk)
There are four mulberry trees planted around one of the
lawns; three are recent but the fourth is said to have been
planted by King James I when he came to visit Robert Cecil.
The story could easily be true and, even if it is not, it adds
to the sense of history of both the garden and the plants.
There is an orchard, originally planted with dwarf trees but
now consisting of half standards as they are tougher. The
grass beneath is full of wildflowers and bulbs, which look
especially lovely in late spring with pale yellow daffodils
and bright blue camassias. The trees themselves have
beautiful metal labels, putting almost all other gardens
to shame. There are also Apple Walks and a fabulous
tunnel of apples in the Kitchen Garden.

Kent

**Brogdale Collections, Brogdale Farm, Brogdale Road,
Faversham, ME13 8XZ**.
Tel 01795 536250 (www.brogdalecollections.org)
This is the world's largest collection of fruit varieties, with
the National Collections of apples and pears and more
cherries, plums, medlars and quinces than most other gardens.
The trees are planted in pairs, with wildflowers beneath,
which helps to make this much more than simply a place
of research. The blossom is staggered from late March to May,
and throughout that time somewhere in the garden will be a
profusion of pink or white flowers. The collections are equally
impressive later in the year when the trees are laden with
fruit. There are various fruit days held throughout the year.

Penshurst Place, Penshurst, TN11 8DG.
Tel 01892 870307 (www.penshurstplace.com)
The gardens were originally laid out in the mid-16th-century
and, in the 19th-century, divided into a series of 'rooms'
with yew hedges. Many of the older features survive, such
as a large espalier which grows on the old wall and spreads
out either side of the newer yew hedge. There is an
atmospheric orchard with wildflowers, mown paths and
seats, but there are fruit trees literally everywhere in the
garden. They line the back of the flower borders, they grow
through the trellises intermingled with roses, clematis and
honeysuckle, and they provide the structure for the knot
garden. Some trees are old and gnarled, others are young
and upright; many of all ages are garlanded with mistletoe.

**Sissinghurst Castle Garden, Sissinghurst, nr Cranbrook,
TN17 2AB.**
Tel 01580 710700 (National Trust)
There is an orchard of apple and cherry trees. The orchard
trees were old when the Nicolsons came to Sissinghurst in
1930s, and may have been planted 100 years earlier to feed
the parish poor who worked the farm. Vita Sackville-West
trained roses such as Madame Plantier through the apple
trees, which may not be particularly practical but is amazingly
pretty. Until the 1960s, the surrounding land consisted of a
mixed farm and this is now being reinstated. An orchard of
apples, plums, pears and cherries has been planted with the
aim of supplying the restaurant and shop at the garden.

Lincolnshire

**Woolsthorpe Manor, Water Lane, Woolsthorpe by
Colsterworth, nr Grantham, NG33 5PD**.

Tel 01476 862823 (National Trust)

This is not an extensive garden but it was the home of Sir
Isaac Newton and was where the famous apple fell. The
original apple tree apparently blew down in 1820, but there
is an old tree in the orchard which is said to have grown up
from the fallen trunk. There are Apple Day celebrations.

Norfolk

Felbrigg Hall, Norwich, NR11 8PR.

Tel 01263 837444 (National Trust)

There is a proper working kitchen garden here with fruit trees
beautifully trained around the walls. In front of the pretty
dovecote there are Norfolk Royal Russet apple trees trained in
pyramids, which look lovely in both spring with the blossom
and autumn with the bright red, russety fruit. There is also an
orchard with some old full-size trees and bee hives to complete
the picture of charming productiveness.

Northants

Canons Ashby House, Daventry, NN11 3SD.
Tel 01327 861900 (National Trust)
This is a very charming and rather romantic 18th-century formal garden. There is an orchard of apple and pear trees and there are old varieties of espaliered pears. To complete the romance of the garden, Spenser wrote part of *The Faerie Queene* here.

Northumberland

Cragside, Rothbury, Morpeth, NE65 7PX.
Tel 01669 620333 (National Trust)
Immediately around the house there is a craggy, almost Gothic garden, but half a mile away there are three formal terraces. One has a large orchard house which contains mostly tender fruit trees but is fascinating as the pots are rotated on turntables to ensure even growth.

Surrey

Royal Horticultural Society Garden, Wisley, GU23 6QB
Tel 01483 224234 (www.rhs.org.uk)
The orchards here extend over a massive hillside. It was too windy for the National Collections (see Brogdale and Norton Priory) but there is a huge variety of fruit trees, both free-standing and intricately trained. There is a very charming quince orchard with a mixture of old gnarled trees and new specimens. There are fruit courses and Apple Day celebrations.

Sussex

Bateman's, Bateman's Lane, Burwash, TN19 7DS.
Tel 01435 882302 (National Trust)
Rudyard Kipling lived here from 1902 until his death in 1936, and designed most of the garden himself. There is a pear allee and a small orchard of mixed fruit trees with lovely views over the house and garden. The tree in the centre of the Mulberry Lawn is young and very small, but, with a little imagination, you can sense what it must have looked like and, indeed, will look like again in a few years.

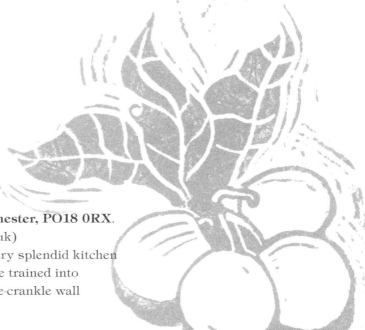

West Dean Gardens, West Dean, Chichester, PO18 0RX.
Tel 01243 818210 (www.westdean.org.uk)
The jewel here is the immaculate and very splendid kitchen
garden. In the orchard, the fruit trees are trained into
interesting shapes, and there is a crinkle-crankle wall
lined with fruit.

Yorkshire
Beningborough Hall, Beningborough, York, YO30 1DD.
Tel 01904 472027 (National Trust)
In the centre of the extensive kitchen garden is a pear allee,
dating from 1827. The old varieties include Pitmaston
Duchess, Clapp's Favourite, Beurre Hardy and Black
Worcester, and are underplanted with herbs. There are
Apple Day celebrations.

Nunnington Hall, Nunnington, nr York, YO62 5UY.
Tel 01439 748283 (National Trust)
A charming garden on the River Rye. In the 19th-century,
the area specialised in producing long-storing apples for
sailing ships, and the orchard has been replanted with these
varieties, including Dog's Snout, Cockpit and Burr Knot.

Wales
Erdigg, Wrexham, Clwyd, LL13 0YT.
Tel 01978 355314 (National Trust)
The 18th-century formal design has survived, despite a
monumental restoration programme. Fruit trees were an
important part of this design, and there are apples, pears and
plums arranged in quincunxes with neatly trimmed pyramids
and espaliers. There is also an orchard with many varieties
dating from the 17th-century. There are Apple Day celebrations.

Scotland

Culross Palace, Culross, Dunfermline, Fife, KY12 8JH.
Tel 01383 880359 (National Trust for Scotland)
This is an organic garden which was restored in the 1990s
but retains a strong 17th-century feel. The walled kitchen
and ornamental garden is terraced and brims with plants of all
types. Trained apples, pears and cherries mingle with jasmine
and roses along the walls. There is also an orchard with Scots
Dumpy chickens pecking contentedly beneath the trees.

Fyvie Castle, Turriff, Aberdeenshire, AB53 8JS.
Tel 01651 891266 (National Trust for Scotland)
There has been a kitchen garden here since at least 1777,
but the current garden is a recent design to celebrate Scottish
fruit and vegetables. A comprehensive apple collection is planned
with varieties on different rootstocks and trained in different
shapes. Pears and plums are trained along the south-facing wall.

Priorwood Garden, Melrose, Borders, TD6 9PZ.
Tel 01896 209504 (National Trust for Scotland)
Built within the precinct of Melrose Abbey, this is a *'spacious
town garden....that behaves as if it were a country estate.'* The
orchard is a mixture of old and new varieties designed to show
the history of apples in Britain since the Romans. There are
picnic tables amongst the grass, with some lovely old large
trees of apples, pears, plums and medlars. There are Apple
Day celebrations.

**Threave Garden, Castle Douglas, Dumfries & Galloway,
DG7 1RX**.
Tel 01556 502575 (National Trust for Scotland)
This has been a school of horticulture since 1960 and is very

much a working garden. The walled garden has apples as small trees and cordons, and beautiful fan-trained pears. In the orchard, there is a collection of old Scottish pears gathered from orchards in Dundee and Perth.

IRELAND
Ardgillan Castle and Garden, Balbriggan, Co Dublin.
Tel (1) 849 2219 (www.ardgillancastle.ie)
It is worth visiting this garden for the spectacular views from the approach road alone. Part of the walled garden is laid out with ornamental fruit, and there is a free-standing wall with twenty alcoves to protect fruit trees.

Glenveagh Castle, Church Hill, Letterkenny, Co. Donegal.
Tel +353 76 100 2537 (www.glenveaghnationalpark.ie)
This is a splendid late 19th-century castle overlooking Lough Veagh. The kitchen garden contains a good selection of local Irish apples.

FRANCE
Chateau de la Guyonniere, 79420, Beaulieu-sous-Parthenay (west of Poitiers).
A charming turreted 14th-century chateau with a medieval-style garden and orchard.

Jardin du Luxembourg, Paris.
(www.gardenvisit.com/garden/jardin_du_luxembourg)
This was a royal palace until the Revolution, when it then became a prison. In 1801 it was used for the Senate, and in the 19th-century the gardens were redesigned as a public park. Despite all these changes, much of the original formal 18th-century design survives, with more than 200 apples and pears beautifully trained in fans and espaliers.

Above: This orchard, at Fenton House, London, may be small, but it is an oasis of tranquility.

Potager du Roi, Chateau de Versailles, Versailles.
(www.chateauversailles.fr)
This was laid out between 1678–83 by Jean-Baptiste de La Quintinie for Louis XIV. Like everything else at Versailles the twenty-two acres of kitchen garden was a display of royal power, as well as a productive garden. It remains almost unaltered and, although none of the original trees survive (contrary to popular belief), many of the 5,000 trees are varieties such as Winter Bon Chrétien which Quintinie used. All the trees are immaculately pruned into shapes, including goblets, pyramids, espaliers and fans.

Potager et Verger Conservatoire du Musee du Revermont, Cuisat, 01370 Treffort, Ain.
(www.musees.paysdelain.fr)
Local and interesting varieties of fruit within the museum site.

Domaine de Saint-Jean de Beauregard, Rue de Château, 91940 Saint-Jean de Beauregard, Île de France.
(www.chateaudesaintjeandebeauregard.com)
There is a delightful walled garden, richly planted with fruit, vegetables and flowers. Pear trees line the paths, and there are trained trees with sculptures and wacky scarecrows in between. There is an annual Fêtes des Plantes.

Jardins Ethnobotaniques de la Gardie, Ancienne École de Pont'd'Avène, 30340 Rousson (Gard).
(www.lesjardinsethno.org)
A series of separate gardens, one of which is a conservation orchard with interesting varieties. There is also a meadow and beekeeping garden.

BELGIUM
Kruidentuin Hortus Botanicus Leuven, Leuven, nr Brussels.
(www.gardenvisit.com/garden/kruidentuin_leuven)
The beautiful botanic garden includes a fruit garden with impeccably trained trees.

Castle of Gaasbeek, Lennik, Vlaams Brabant.
(www.castelvangaasbeek.be)
The castle itself is a national museum, but the surrounding park contains an amazing amount of beautifully trained fruit.

HOLLAND
Slot Zuylen, nr Utrecht.
(www.slotzuylen.nl/english)
This is a moated castle which had an extensive orchard in the 17th-century and formal gardens in the 18th. Both have changed over the years but there are still ancient espaliered pear trees with gnarled trunks, and two attractive orchards.

Kasteel-Museum Sypesteyn, Loosdrecht.
(www.sypesteyn.nl)
The romantic castle was built in the 19th-century and is
surrounded by a formal 17th-century garden. There is a pear
pergola and, across the moat, an orchard with quince and
walnut trees planted in 1999.

Menkemaborg, CV Uithuizen.
(www.menkemaborg.nl)
The garden has been reconstructed from a plan of 1705,
and the kitchen garden has a pear tunnel and an orchard
of old apple varieties.

ITALY
**Archelogia Arborea, San Lorenzo di Lerchi, Citta di
Castello, Perugia.**
(www.archeologiaarborea.org)
This is the collection of Livio Dalla Ragione and his daughter
Isabella. Started in 1960, there are now about 400 apples,
pears, plums, cherries, quinces and medlars. Grafts of the
trees are for sale and there are local fruit shows in Perugia.
The orchards are open by appointment and there is a medieval
guest house which can be rented.

L'Orto dei Frutti Dimenticati, Pennabilli, nr Rimini.
(www.museoiluoghidellanima.it/orto-dei-frutti-dimenticati)
The name translates as 'The Garden of Forgotten Fruits'. This
is one of seven museums in the village. The orchard contains
old varieties, mingling with sculptures. Amongst other local
fruits there are 300 varieties of apple.

Parco Burcina 'Felice Piacenza', Pollone, Piemonte.
(www.atl.biella.it/parco-burcina).
This is a woodland garden in the foothills of the Piemontese
Alps, with a recent collection of old, local varieties of apple.

SWEDEN
Bergianska Trädgården, Stockholm.
(www.bergianska.se).
Stockholm's botanic garden has a well-stocked kitchen garden
with a fruit and berry collection, including forty-five Swedish
apple varieties.

Norrvikens Trädgårdar, Bastad.
(www.norrvikenstradgardar.net)
This is a lovely garden which combines beautiful planting
with interesting sculpture displays. Amongst other things,
there is a mulberry arch and an orchard of cherry trees.

Fredriksdal, Helsingborg.
(www.fredriksdal.se)
A charming, rustic open-air museum with a fruit garden
and an orchard with fifty varieties of Swedish apples.

USA
Boscobel, Garrison, New York.
(www.boscobel.org).
There is an apple orchard which leads through to the herb
garden. Rustic wooden pergolas and trained fruit trees
surround the garden with free-standing trees in the formal
raised beds. There are amazing views over the Hudson River.

Monticello and The Thomas Jefferson Center for Historic Plants, Charlottesville, Virginia.
(www.monticello.org)
Between 1769 and 1814, Thomas Jefferson planted an eight-
acre Fruitery, which included the 400-tree South Orchard.

Above: This gazebo at Monticello, Virginia, USA, is the perfect place to sit and admire the surrounding gardens. Once you have planted your orchard, it is just as important to have somewhere to sit and appreciate it.

A separate North Orchard included cider apples and it is estimated that he planted over a thousand trees in that time. Along with apples, there were innumerable peaches and cherries. The garden fell into disrepair in the late 19th-century but restoration has been comparatively straightforward as Jefferson kept immaculate records of absolutely everything. This garden combines some of the best traditions of the Old World with the finest dynamism of the New.

AUSTRALIA
Huon Apple and Heritage Museum, Grove, Tasmania.
(www.newnorfolk.org/apple-museum)
A museum has been set out in an old packing shed showing how fruit growers lived a hundred years ago. At any time there are up to 500 different varieties of apple on display.

Specialist Nurseries

There are a great many nurseries around the country and, indeed, world that sell fruit trees. The trees should be healthy and the staff knowledgeable. Don't be afraid of asking questions, most will be happy to help, and enjoy being able to discuss the varieties they have with you. Remember, they are often specialists in what they do and take pride in their work. Questions regarding rootstocks and local varieties will soon tell you. Below is a selection of the very best. There are many others all over the country. Always ring before visiting a nursery. Some concentrate on mail order, and are only open on certain days, or by appointment.

ENGLAND
Agroforestry Research Trust, 46 Hunters Moon, Dartington, Totnes, Devon TQ9 6JT. Tel: 01830 840776 www.agroforestry.co.uk (Mail order only.)

Bernwode Plants, Kingswood lane, Ludgershall, Bucks HP18 9RB. Tel: 01844 237415 www.bernewodeplants.co.uk

Blackmoor Nurseries, Blackmoor Estate, Blackmoor, Liss, Hampshire GU33 6BS. Tel: 01420 473576 www.blackmoor.co.uk

Bridgemere Nurseries, Bridgemere, nr Nantwich, Cheshire CW5 7QB. Tel: 01270 521100 www.bridgemere.co.uk (No mail order.)

Chris Bowers and Sons, Whispering Trees Nurseries, Wimbotsham, Norfolk PE43 3QB. Tel: 01366 388752 www.chrisbowers.co.uk

Clay Barn Orchard, Fingringhoe, nr Colchester, Essex. Tel: 01260 735405

Crown Nursery, High Street, Ufford, Woodbridge, Suffolk IP13 6EL. Tel: 01394 460755. www.crown-nursery.co.uk

Grow at Brogdale, Brogdale Road, Faversham, Kent ME13 8XZ. Tel: 01795 531888 www.brogdaleonline.co.uk

Deacon's Nursery, Moor View, Godshill, Isle of Wight PO38 3HW. Tel: 01983 840750 www.deaconsnurseryfruits.co.uk

Endsleigh Gardens Nursery, Milton Abbot, Tavistock, Devon PL19 0PG. Tel: 01822 870235 www.endsleigh-garden.com

Highfields Nursery, Church Lane, Little Tey, Colchester, CO6 1HX. Tel: 01206 212325 www.highfieldsnursery.co.uk (Wholesale)

Keepers Nursery, Gallants Court, Gallants Lane, East Farleigh, Maidstone, Kent ME15 0LE. Tel: 01622 726465 www.keepers-nursery.co.uk

Ken Muir, Honeypot Farm, Rectory Road, Weeley Heath, Clacton-on-Sea, Essex CO16 9BJ. Tel: 0870 7479222 www.kenmuir.co.uk

Southern Fruit Trees, Old Grain Dryer Corner, Blackmoor, Liss, GU33 6BP. Tel: 01420 488822 www.southernfruittrees.co.uk

Walcot Organic Nursery, Lower Walcot Farm, Walcot Lane, Drakes Broughton, Worcestershire WR10 2AL. Tel: 01905 841587 www.walcotnursery.co.uk

Thornhayes Nursery, St Andrews Wood, Dulford,
Cullompton, Devon EX15 2DF. Tel: 01884 266746
www.thornhayes-nursery.co.uk

SCOTLAND
Butterworth's Organic Nursery, Garden Cottage, Auchinleck
Estate, Camnock, Ayrshire KA18 2LR. Tel: 01290 551088
(By appointment only.)

Tweedie Fruit Trees, Maryfield Road Nursery, near
Terragles, Dumfriesshire, DG2 9TH. Tel: 01387 720880

WALES
Dolau-hirion Fruit Tree Nursery, Capel Isaac, Llandeilo,
Carmarthernshire SA19 7TG. Tel: 01558 668744
www.applewise.co.uk

IRELAND
Future Forests, Ballingeary Road, Kealkin, Bantry, Co Cork.
Tel: 00 353 (0)27 66176 www.futureforsets.ie

PICK-YOUR-OWN
There are masses of pick-your-own farms to visit. If you
particularly want orchard fruits, check beforehand, as many
concentrate on soft fruits only. The two below both have a
good selection of fruit trees.

Maynards Farm, Windmill Hill/Cross Lane, Wadhurst, East
Sussex, TN5 7HQ. Tel: 01580 200394
www.maynardsfruit.co.uk

Garsons, Winterdown Road, West End, Esher, Surrey KT10
8LS. Tel: 01372 464389 www.garsons.co.uk Also at Fontly
Road, Titchfield, Hampshire PO15 6QX

Events

Fruit festivals usually have tastings of local varieties and, quite apart from being great fun, they are useful if you want advice on which varieties to choose. The dates of many of these festivals vary from year to year to fit around weekends. The Royal Horticultural Society and National Trust gardens have celebrations throughout the year; it is worth checking their websites for events. The Common Ground website also has a comprehensive list of events. See page 275.

WASSAILING
This aims to protect the trees from evil spirits and ensure a good crop. It usually takes place on 17th January, the date of Twelfth Night before the introduction of the Gregorian calendar in 1752. The oldest or best tree in the orchard is chosen as Apple Tree Man, or the guardian of the orchard. Cider is poured on the roots, and a piece of toast or cake, soaked in cider, is placed in the branches to attract robins, who are the good spirits of the trees. Guns are fired, or saucepans banged, to scare away any bad spirits and wake the trees, which are then often serenaded with traditional songs. Finally, there are toasts (with more cider) and a good harvest is ensured. The name is thought to come from the Anglo-Saxon *wes hal*, was haile or wase hail, meaning to be in good health.

BLOSSOM DAYS
Blossom starts in March or April and carries right on to mid-May. Many orchards celebrate the blossom and there is a Blossom Route in Worcestershire.

DAMSON DAY

This is celebrated on 13th April in Westmorland when the blossom is at its height.

SEER GREEN CHERRY PIE FAIR

This is one of the most famous cherry fairs and is held on or around 22nd June. The first Sunday in August is traditionally Cherry Pie Sunday in Buckinghamshire.

CHERRY DAY

This is celebrated throughout the country in June or July. Visit the website, www.foodloversbritain.com, then go to Cherry Aid for exact dates each year.

PEAR DAY

Pears ripen between August and November. Canon Hall Museum, near Barnsley in Yorkshire celebrates the harvest on 15th September.

PLUM DAY

Plums ripen in August and September. Pershore College in Worcestershire celebrates Plum Day on August Bank Holiday. Heath Farm in Bluntisham, Cambridgeshire has forty-three varieties of plums, celebrating the harvest in early September.

APPLE DAY

This was started at the Old Apple Market in Covent Garden, London by Common Ground in 1990 and has become the most widely celebrated fruit day. The official date is 21st October, but celebrations are usually held on the surrounding weekends.

QUINCE FESTIVAL

This usually takes place on the first weekend in October at Norton Priory in Cheshire.

Glossary

BIENNIAL BEARING: Many fruit trees have a habit of only producing a significant crop every other year (for example, Ellison's Orange apples are notorious for this). You can improve this situation by carefully reducing the crop in the good year, pruning sensibly, and making sure the tree is properly fed and watered.

BUD, FRUIT: Most orchard trees produce different types of bud. Those that are going to turn into blossom, and subsequently fruit, are round and plump – if you take them all off the previous year, you won't get much fruit the next!

BUD, LEAF: Buds that are going to turn into new stalks and leaves tend to be longer and thinner than fruit buds.

CULTIVAR: Although there are botanical differences between 'cultivars' and 'varieties', you can use either word when talking about fruit trees to mean, in practice, a recognisable type of a particular fruit that is sufficiently well known to be regularly grown and propagated. The name will usually be contained in single inverted commas (for example the apple 'Ashmead's Kernel'), but for the purposes of this book the inverted commas have been omitted for clarity and space. By some reckonings there may be as many as 8,000 different varieties or cultivars of apple (not many are common, or necessarily even any good), but far fewer of pears, cherries, plums, medlars, mulberries and quinces.

GRAFTING: Many orchard fruit trees, and especially apples, cannot be grown from seed (their pips or stones) to, in any way, resemble their parents, so to keep them true to type and produce high-quality fruit, gardeners have evolved a way of reproducing

Opposite left: The fat, lower buds, are the fruit buds which will turn into blossom and then fruit. The thinner buds are leaf buds, which will grow into leaves and, eventually, branches. 'A' shows a tip bearer, and 'B' shows a spur bearer. The differences are important when it comes to pruning.

Opposite right: The rootstock is the part of the tree below ground, which largely determines the size of the tree. The part above ground is the scion, and determines the type of fruit and general appearance of the tree. 'A' shows the leader, or dominant central stem. The right-hand detail shows the graft, or point where the two join. It is important that the tree is planted with this part above ground level.

them called grafting. A bit of the old tree is carefully joined onto a rootstock (stem and root system) of a suitably sized and compatible tree, so that they will grow together as one plant. Apples are usually grafted onto other apples, but pears, for example, are sometimes grafted onto quince rootstocks. Although it is not as difficult to do this as many books and experts imply, you would want to have grown fruit for a few years before you try.

LEADER: When most orchard trees grow naturally they tend to have a dominant central stem that grows straight up towards the sky – the leader. Leaving this in place may result in a tree that is too tall for many owners, and whose fruit is harder to gather. Therefore, it is often cut out as part of the pruning required to train the young tree, into, for example, a bush shape, in the early years of its life. You don't need to be frightened about doing this, but it helps to have a clear idea of the shape of tree you eventually want before you start cutting!

POLLINATION: To get a successful fruit crop, pollen needs to be transferred (usually by bees) between one flower and another, and then succeed in fertilising the flower it reaches. In the case of most apple trees, the pollen needs to come from different varieties of apple, including crab-apples. Some very good modern apples can, however, use their own pollen to fertilise their flowers, and are known as self-fertile (Greensleeves and Queen Cox, for example). Many plums, cherries and pears also require pollen from different varieties to produce good fruit, but most quinces, medlars and mulberries do not. Take advice from a specialist nurseryman!

ROOTSTOCK: This is the 'in the ground bit' of the tree to which the 'top bit' of the tree you want to propagate (make another one of) is joined. It will usually, subject to soil and growing conditions, determine the overall size, and influence the disease resistance of the new tree. Rootstocks have been carefully produced in a number of standard, disease-resistant types, often known by a rather confusing system of numbers and letters (e.g. M9). Again, take advice from a specialist nurseryman when you buy!

SCION: This old-fashioned word means the 'top bit' of a grafted tree that keeps the variety or cultivar constant throughout many different generations. The scion or 'scion wood' will determine the type of fruit it bears and its general appearance

SPUR: Many fruit trees produce their fruit buds, and subsequent fruit, on short stubby spurs along the stems and that develop over a period of years. Accordingly, SPUR BEARERS are those trees that produce all or most of their fruit in this way. When you prune a tree of this sort, you need to strike a balance between keeping the old spurs, and encouraging the growth of new branches in the right places.

TIP BEARER: Alternatively, some fruit trees (such as the apple Cornish Gillyflower) produce all, or most of their fruit, from fruit buds at the end of their stems. If you cut all the ends off this type of tree to tidy it up, you will seriously reduce your crop.

TRIPLOID: Nearly all animals and most plants have two full sets of genetic materials (chromosomes), but some have more. Several varieties of orchard fruits have three (or very occasionally four) sets. Those with three sets (such as Bramley and Blenheim Orange apples) are known as triploids. Their pollen is usually very bad at fertilising, either their own flowers or those of other varieties of the same fruit, so you need to make sure that the pollen is available from somewhere else. You could use a crab apple, or, in theory, a single self-fertile apple that flowers at the same time as your triploid, or two normal apples that flower at the same time (that way they can fertilise each other since the triploid won't do the job!).

Bibliography

GENERAL
The *Common Ground Book of Orchards*, Common Ground
    (Common Ground, 2000)
Jane Grigson's Fruit Book, Jane Grigson (latest edition: Penguin
    Books, 2000)
The Duchess of Malfi's Apricots and Other Literary Fruits, Robert
    Palter (University of South Carolina Press, 2002)
Forgotten Fruit, Christopher Stocks (Windmill Books, 2009)

HISTORY
The Anatomy of Dessert, Edward Bunyard (latest edition: Modern
    Library Series, Random House USA, 2006)
New Orchard and Garden with the Country Housewifes Garden,
    William Lawson (edited Malcolm Thick, facsimile of 1617 edition,
    Prospect Books, 2003)
The Oxford Companion to the Garden, Patrick Taylor (Oxford
    University Press, 2008)

GARDENING
Growing Fruit, Harry Baker (Octopus Publishing Group, 1999)
The Fruit Expert, D. G. Hessayon (series Expert Books, Transworld
    Publishers Ltd, 2006)
Grow Your Own Fruit, Carol Klein (Octopus Publishing Group,
    imprint Mitchell Beazley, 2009)

GARDENS
Yellow Book: NGS Gardens Open for Charity (The National Gardens
    Scheme, published annually)

APPLES

The Apple Source Book, Sue Clifford and Angela King
(Hodder and Stoughton, 2008)

Apple Games and Customs, Common Ground (Common Ground, 1994)

The Story of the Apple, Barrie Juniper and David Mabberley (Timber Press, 2006)

The New Book of Apples: The Definitive Guide to Over 2,000 Varieties, Joan Morgan and Alison Richards (Ebury Press, 2002)

ILLUSTRATED

Pomona Britannica, George Brookshaw (Taschen Press, 2005)

Websites

www.commonground.org.uk

All aspects relating to the countryside and its preservation. Fruit days, celebrations and local customs.

www.rhs.org.uk

Royal Horticultural Society

www.nationaltrust.org.uk/www.nts.org.uk

The National Trust/The National Trust for Scotland

www.ngs.org.uk

The National Gardens Scheme or 'Yellow Book'. Mostly private gardens open on specific days.

www.wfga.org.uk

The Women's Farm and Garden Association runs some very good hands-on courses for its members on cultivating orchard fruit, including pruning.

Index

Page numbers in *italic* indicate a picture or its caption. Page numbers in **bold** indicate a main section. Recipes are all listed under **Recipes** (R section).

B
Babycham 121
Baljon, Lodewijk 70
Ballerina types *19*, 72
Ballindoolin (Co. Kildare) 258
bare-rooted trees 218
Barge Gardens (London) 244
Bartlett, Enoch 113
Bateman's (Sussex) 70, 253
Beatles 98–9
beauty products, quinces for 143
bees in orchards *63*, 64, *212–13*
Bellini 138
Beningbrough Hall (Yorkshire)
  68, 70, 253, 256
Bergianska Trädgården (Sweden)
  262
Berrington Hall (Hereford &
  Worcs) 247
biennial bearing 231, 270
Binning, Lord 41
bird problems 231
Blackmore, R D 119–20
Blossom Days 268
bobbing for apples *93*
Boccaccio 114, 119
Boscobel (New York) 262
Boucher, François *171*
Brailsford, Mary Anne 85
Brecht, Bertholt 159
British orchards: history 28–49
Brogdale Horticulrual Trust
  (Kent) 8, 48, 249
Broussonetia papyrifera see
  mulberries, paper
brown rot 230
buddleja to attract wildlife 225
buds
  fruit 270, *271*
  leaf 270, *271*
bulbs for wildflower meadow
  229
Bull, Dr Henry 87
bullaces 12–13, 150–1
  choosing 56
  taxonomy 209
Bulmer, Rev. Charles 87
Bunyard, Dr A 12, 102, 114, 122

C
calvados 99
Campion, Sir Thomas 176–7
campion for wildflower meadow
  229
canker 230
Canons Ashby House
  (Northamptonshire) 13, 252

Canterbury Monastery 29
Canterbury Tales (Chaucer) 94,
  119, 190
Caro, Sir Anthony 91
Castelvetro, Giacomo 191
Cato 110
Cezanne 94
Chaenomeles 57
Chardin 92–4, 159
Charles I, King 34
Charles V, King 171
Charlottesville *see* Monticello
  Gardens (USA)
Chateau de la Guyonnière
  (France) 258
Chaucer 119, 140, 190
Chekhov 177
Chelsea Physic Garden 202
chemicals 230
cherries **166–83**
  Amarelle 168–9
  in art 175
  black 181
  blossom *174–5*, 177
  botanic drawing *166*
  choosing 56
  culinary aspects 15
  diseases 224
  double *178*, 179
  drinks 180
  Dukes (Royales) 169
  in flower gardens 69
  glacé 181
  growing *see* fruit trees, growing
  harvesting 232
  for health 179–80
  history 14–15, 169–75
  in literature 175–7
  Marasca 180
  maraschino 181
  Mayduke 241
  Morello 14, 56, *75*, 168–9, 241
  ornamental 169
  Ponticum 169
  pruning 224
  ripe *172–3*, *178*
  rootstocks 174, 215
  sour 14, 181
    taxonomy 209
  Stella 241
  Sunburst 241
  as symbols 15, 177, 179
  taxonomy 209
  types 168–9
  varieties 241
  wild 168
  wood from 179

cherruzerd 174
Cherry Aid 175
cherry brandy 180
Cherry Day 175, 269
cherry fairs/festivals 177
The Cherry Orchard (Chekhov)
  177
cherry plum 150, 151
Cherry Robbers (Lawrence) 179
cherry spitting 177
Cherry Tree Carol 176
chickens in orchards *59*, 63, 67
Chinese apples 39
chives as companion plants
  224
cider brandy 99
cider industry 81, 82, 87, 99,
  100–1
Clay Barn Orchard (Essex) *46*
Clifford, Sue 90
climbers through fruit trees 69
Cobbett, William 191
Cockney language 120
Commentaries (Plutarch) 136
commercial fruit growing 41–5
Common Ground charity 46, 90
companion planting 226–30
container-grown fruit 8, 74, 218,
  221, 221–2
  rootstocks 215
cordons 71, *73*
  rootstocks 215
  spacing trees 216
cornflower
  for wildflower meadow 229
  to attract wildlife 225, *225*
courtly orchards 29
cow parsley as companion plants
  224
Cox, Mr 85
crab apples
  in flower gardens 69
  history 81–2
  taxonomy 209
Cragside (Northumberland)
  252
Cranach the Elder, Lucas *91*
cranesbill, meadow, for
  wildflower meadow 229
The Creation (Caro) 91
Culpeper, Nicholas 143, 179,
  180, 190–1
Culross Palace (Fife) 256
cultivars 270
culture *see under specific fruit*
Cydonia see quinces

Picture credits

Pg 7 © GAP Photos/FhF
Greenmedia; **Pg 9** © akg-
images/Gilles Mermet; **Pg 10-11**
© Gap Photos/Marg Cousens;
Pg 12-13 © Photolibrary/Garden
Picture Library/Juliette Wade; **Pg
15** © Gap Photos/Juliette Wade;
Pg 16-17 © Alamy/John Miller;
Pg 19 © Gap Photos/ Friedrich
Strauss; Pg **20-21** © Clive
Nichols/Chateau Plaisir,
France/Designer: Pascal Cribier.
Pg 22-23 © Corbis/Scott Barrow;

Pg 24 © The Bridgeman Art
Library/Egyptian National
Museum, Cairo, Egypt; **Pg 25** ©
The Bridgeman Art Library/The
Stapleton Collection/Private
Collection; **Pg 26** © Mary Evans
Picture Library; **Pg 32** © Gap
Photos/Heather Edwards; **Pg 35**
© The Bridgeman Art
Library/The Stapleton
Collection/Private Collection;
Pg 36 © The Bridgeman Art
Library/Private Collection/Sophie

Grandval, The King's Vegetable
Garden at Versailles; **Pg 42-43** ©
Monticello/Thomas Jefferson
Foundation, Inc; **Pg 44** © Gap
Photos/John Glover; **Pg 47** © ph
Christian Barnett/Country Living
© The National Magazine Company
Ltd; **Pg 49** © The Bridgeman Art
Library/Fitzwilliam Museum,
University of Cambridge, UK;
Pg 50-51 © Gap Photos/Geoff du
Feu; **Pg 52** © Clive Nichols/Clare
Matthews; **Pg 54-55** © Gap

Acknowledgments

We would both like to thank all the owners of and gardeners at the orchards we have visited recently and especially all the specialist staff at Brogdale and RHS Wisley.

JANE: Firstly, I must thank Sue Dunster for rekindling my love of orchards with her love of quinces. Sue Gibb has been a great support, both on a practical front and as company on the many 'necessary' outings. Paul Honor, yet again, rescued me innumerable times from computer catastrophe. Matt Hopkins, Valerie Scriven, Karin Scherer, Barry Delves and Louy Carpenter have all provided help and encouragement, for which I am very grateful. I would never have completed my recipes without the help of my testers, Libby Kerr, and Eric Treuille, Sally Hughes, Camille Rope, Marilou Amante and Shelley McGlashen at Books for Cooks. And last, but not least, thanks to my testers par excellence; Claire Harris and Matthew Crockatt.

CHRIS: I fondly remember our old gardener Tom Holman, who taught me such practical skills as I may possess.

BOTH: We would never have got this project off the ground without the support of our agent, Teresa Chris, who provided a perfect balance of encouragement and advice. At Pavilion Anna Cheifetz and Katie Deane have been brilliant to work with. Our picture editor, Emma O'Neill has been amazing at sourcing everything we asked for, and more, and Georgie Hewitt, the designer, has arranged it all beautifully. Between them, Emma Jane Frost and Nicki Dowey made our recipes look amazing. Thank you all.

Finally, we would like to thank each other. Writing can be a lonely business but writing this book has been immense fun right from the start.

This edition published in the United Kingdom in 2019 by
Pavilion Books
43 Great Ormond Street
London
WC1N 3HZ

First edition published in 2010

ISBN: 978-1-911624-77-6

A CIP catalogue record for this book is available from the
British Library.

10 9 8 7 6 5 4 3 2 1

Reproduction by Mission Productions, Hong Kong
Printed and bound by Toppan Leefung Printing Ltd, China

www.pavilionbooks.com